THE
VEILED PULSE
OF TIME

THE
VEILED PULSE
OF TIME

An Introduction to

Biographical Cycles and Destiny

William Bryant

Ø Anthroposophic Press

Published in the United States by Anthroposophic Press,
R.R. 4, Box 94 A-1, Hudson, New York 12534.

Library of Congress Cataloging-in-Publication Data

Bryant,William, 1933–
    The veiled pulse of time : an introduction to biographical cycles
and destiny / by William Bryant.
    Includes bibliographical references.
    ISBN 0-88010-374-4 (pbk.)
    1. Rhythm.   2. Life cycle, Human.   3. Celebrities—Biography.
4. Anthroposophy.   I. Title.
BP596.R5B78   1993
299'.935—dc20   93–25934

Cover design: Barbara Richey

10 9 8 7 6 5 4 3 2 1

Printed in the United States of America

Contents

Introduction

"What am I? I am my life. All my life is my Time."
—Maurice Nicoll, *Living Time*

Since my childhood I have been fascinated by the way people navigate the course between birth and death. Frequent spells of illness in my early years severely restricted my participation in the life around me, forcing me to look at the world as a spectator, a reluctant onlooker. But my emerging feelings during this protracted winter of childhood were more than a mixture of physical discomfort, shyness, and fear. I remember watching the comings and goings of aunts, uncles, grandparents, and strangers, and wondering where they had come from, where they were going, and why. This sense of wonder did not disperse as I grew up, but firmly seeded itself somewhere in my psyche to engender my love for biography. Looking back, I think I dimly suspected even then that every person has his personal allotment of Time, a time life containing the secrets of his own life story.

The most disquieting thing about my early perceptions of life, perhaps magnified by the Second World War, was the unexpected disruptions, the dramatic intrusions which strike without warning. When later I looked into history and the life of civilizations, nations, and societies, I saw this same confusion—periods of chaos and creation, ascent and decline. To me, the events which tore the tranquility of individuals to shreds seemed to be the most frighteningly impressive thing about this strange world. Crises come and go, but undoubtedly they present a fundamental problem for all of us.

As a youth I thought that life would be a monstrous thing unless submerged beneath its surface were the wellsprings of new creation and some kind of cohesive, meaningful design and structure. I knew that if I could recognize purpose in my crises, then the traumas of existence would offer me a better chance for renewal and growth rather than disenchantment and destructive despair.

Our biography is our most precious and intimate possession, yet how many of us can make head or tail of it? How much do we really know about ourselves and our involvement in the complex construction of our own life story? Psychology tells us that we have a Self, a center that we call "I." But our waking mind, stumbling its way through time as if suspended in a dream, barely detects its presence, let alone its influence on our yesterdays and tomorrows.

The problem, as I see it, is time. I appear to live on the infinitely small island of time I call *now*. But this infinitesimal spot of semicertainty, this present moment separating my before from my after, appears to be all that my waking mind can truly experience of its own reality. Despite this mental barrier, something in me is convinced that I am greater, richer, deeper, and more real than my shriveled experience of myself in these single moments. Whatever is real about me casts its presence behind and before me, which memory glimpses as my past and intuition senses as my future. Thus, I can feel in my life some sort of direction infinitely more important than a mere succession of conscious moments. This sense of direction is the key to the meaning of my existence, my destiny in the world of time and space. In other words, the meaning of my life and the succession of events and experiences are contained in the same mystery.

I believe the meaning of our journey through time can be found within biography itself, in the unmistakable patterns which structure its "becoming," its movement toward completion. Perhaps this is one reason why we are so attracted to the life stories of others. Something in our soul responds to biography which helps us to sense meaning and direction in the bewildering changeableness of our own life in time. This interest in the fortunes and misfortunes of others is no less evident in village or office gossip than in an abstract critical analysis of the life and work of a great individual. Reading others' life stories turns their years into our minutes, thereby allowing us to "share" their path in a mere fraction of the time they took to travel it. Biography, in a sense, liberates us from our confinement in the present; by lifting others' lives out of their time, we can better sense the procession of events and changes and recognize how one incident is connected to another. Unlike them, we will not be riveted to each present moment; everything to them was either yesterday, today, or tomorrow, but to us their time is an objective *process*. Thus, we can value the unique placement of each experience in the process of their becoming—something we find extremely difficult to recognize in our own lives.

Biography, then, strengthens our faith in the continuity of our own life, showing us that everyone has a path to travel. But reviewing others' lives is more than mere observation, because we *feel something*—we participate in them. We draw our own parallels, place ourselves in their predicaments and crises, judge their responses and share their suffering and hope. Reading biography is a form of self-knowledge and affirmation.

Of course, we do not need a biographical book, movie, or play to stir our time-sense since we daily come across situations which touch our sense of destiny. Take for example, the quite ordinary experience of waiting to see one's doctor. What about the dishevelled old fellow shuffling his way to the nearest waiting-room chair? One glance will reveal the ruthless handiwork of time which has twisted his anatomy, creased his countenance, and watered his eyes. We may be moved by a passing flutter of pity, even fear or compassion, but do we not wonder about his life story and the untold incidents which have shaped it? We know he is nearing the end of his adventure, his lover's quarrel with time. So full of yesterdays but with only a handful of tomorrows, he has almost spent his ration of time. He is all *past*, yet he *is* and bears within himself all his hopes, fears, and errors, his arguments and reconciliations with life, his achievements and goals. His almost spectral presence proclaims the unspoken truth that we are siblings in time. Soon he will free himself from its remorseless treadmill while we remain its prisoner, for he is the mirror showing us that we are unfinished creatures with more of time to come. His trembling fingers and uncertain tread, however, are nothing less than a terrible deception. Our mental images and value judgements touch nothing of his true reality, for he is above all else a *time being*. He is *all* his time, not merely the moment in which we judge him ready for the scrap heap. Yes, this old tenant of passing time has his own story, and this is his most precious possession—a priceless treasury of experience which neither time nor we can take from him. To know him, we must know his *story*.

Let us pass from the waiting room to the pub! What about that bleary, middle-aged alcoholic slouched in a corner of befuddlement, his destiny becalmed on a sea of booze? Where did he come from and where will he go? What travail has brought about this perilous loss of self? Will his future suffering, germinating before our very eyes, inevitably compel him to face himself? This disquieting prospect of a fellow traveler in time losing his grip on himself naturally fills us with dismay, since losing one's hold on oneself is the same as losing one's foothold in time. Obviously, the solution to his personal problems cannot be instantaneous; it has to work itself out as a process in time. To know the real cause and the results we must know his life story from beginning to end. Our retinal images and emotional discomfort show us nothing of his full reality, only a dismal moment in the vast spread of his immortality.

Few things strike us with more horror, compassion, and wonder than the sight of a soul wriggling on the hook of time, all lashings and contortions as it wrestles its way through its death and rebirth crisis. Similarly, we are moved by wonder, perhaps envy, when a soul climbs to a high summit of success, or when life inexplicably bestows a boon of great fortune.

While we are considering the almost magical influence biography seems to have on the soul, we should not ignore its kinship with history. To say that both represent a process unfolding in time is to state the obvious, but surely it is the unquenchable vitality of biography which keeps history fresh and meaningful by appealing to our sense of path. Ravaged by upheaval and change, the cracked fresco, dusty tome, and battered sword nevertheless reveal fragments of our ancestors' stories. We explore the tyrants, crackpots, and heroes of the past with a touch of personal involvement, no matter how weird their attitudes, conduct, and consciousness. Their stories remind us that each personal page belongs to the greater narrative of its group, nation, and civilization.

Perhaps this affinity between our present and their past exists because we recognize in them a reflection of our own emergence, striving, and pain, our track through time. This "sense of path" is indispensable if we are to relate our own little story to the confusion we call civilization. After all, civilizations are living organisms like human beings, only on a more diversified and broader scale; both embody a living process with a definite direction and time structure. The real meaning behind the enigmatic tapestry of history is somehow interlaced with the meaning of our own personal journey through time. We will understand the historical process only by solving the riddles of biography. Biography and history are two faces of the same coin.

I have said that biography, whether historical or contemporary, appeals to our sense of destiny. Destiny is a word which implies that an individual life involves some kind of *intentional* structure. If this assumption is correct, biography is organized according to certain *laws*. We have grown accustomed to the idea that nature belongs to a cosmos of necessity where the working of cause and effect obeys specific rules. Wherever we look in the universe, from the crystalline symmetry of the snow-flake to the immense island galaxies of outer space, we behold the imprint of design, structure, and transformation. The scientist makes observations, marshals facts, establishes a frame of reference, and comes up with a hypothesis, which is then subjected to exhaustive testing before the theoretical law is announced. Obviously, a science without a cosmos is as unthinkable as a cosmos without the order which binds it all together.

But how do *we* fit into this lawful universe? Obviously, our physical-chemical nature obeys specific laws, but our behavior, aspirations, and wanderings appear to be subject to the unfathomable influence of uncertainty and accident. In many respects we appear to be nothing more than marionettes of circumstance. This fatalistic view of our existence is the most terrifying illusion of all, but there is no need for this deception. Only a little concentration is needed to unearth traces of the marvelous patterning of our time life and its laws, laws as real, necessary, and vital as any found in the physical world. I believe we can understand the connection between time, biography, destiny, and history once we have uncovered the dynamic laws of the psyche which are responsible for the order in our lives. A detailed study of the life span, always relating specific events to the whole, will unmask not only certain time laws but also the presence of an extraordinary intelligence moving individuals along their paths of experience. This innate wisdom, this "subliminal intention," so to speak, is the real creator of biography.

Winston Churchill, for one, was convinced that particular experiences in his youth had clearly nurtured him for the crucial events of his later life. But if the past is indeed alive, well, and active somewhere in our psychic makeup, how exactly does it shape our present and future? Once we have a clear view of this time structure in our lives, we can examine the working of *transformation*. Then we will discover how the psyche assimilates and integrates experience to promote future events and experience.

Not only have I come to see biography as a supreme work of art, I am also convinced that a true science of humankind will need a special *morphology* to render the life span fully intelligible. What is real in our being, the spiritual foundation of our personality, can function in the physical world only as a *process* in time. Our personal growth, evolution, development, becoming— call it what you will—can follow its course only when we have entered the stream of successional time. I am not saying that other forms or dimensions of time do not exist or interpenetrate our being, but whatever else human destiny may be, it is certainly part of a process in successional time.

This morphology is far more than an exercise in fact gleaning and analysis. The inner creator of biography and destiny is a consummate artist of the highest order. The observer sees the wrought work created by the invisible, nonphysical elements of intelligent being. We will also require the qualitative powers of imagination and intuition to glimpse the value of each phase and event relative to the life span as a whole. Destiny, incidentally, in the sense I use it, is more than the rigid determinism of genetics or conditioning. We shall deal with these conflicts later. Suffice it to say that a morphology of biography offers us a conscious rapprochement between our human and scientific experience. This gives us a means to recognize that every life incident is a meaningful expression of the Self moving through its time.

Deepening our awareness of time and destiny inevitably alters our attitude toward life. According to Maurice Nicoll, whose brilliant book *Living Time* sets out to change our conception of time, "To see another person apart from our subjective notions and images, to realize another's objective existence, is exactly one of those momentary and genuine experiences which gives us hints of further states of consciousness."

Thus, a sense of path changes us psychologically; it heightens our self-responsibility, deepens our personal relationships, and helps us to view our crises, changes, and sufferings more objectively. This means that our attention, our consciousness, is not completely consumed by the *now*. We have a sense of span and scale which embraces our past and our future. We are not mere creatures of action and reaction. As we intuit the incredible genesis of our biography, fashioning its substance and character on its own frame of time, we move closer to our own reality and the mystery of freedom.

We also look at the lives of others with more tolerance and objectivity. Once we have digested the idea that everyone has somewhere to go and something to accomplish, we can only be amazed and uplifted by people's indefatigable though unconscious commitment to following a path hidden to them. We know that an orderly process lies hidden behind the distressing problems which appear to be so harsh and unfathomable.

I hope, therefore, that this book will offer a draught of courageous affirmation to the wounded in spirit, whose sense of direction and purpose has been smothered by despair or upheaval. All too often, change comes uninvited to throw our peace and certainty into doubt and confusion. The natural order decrees that there be intervals of vitality and creativity and intervals of withdrawal and suffering. But there is no reason to suppose that such cycles of increase and decrease deprive our lives of meaning and purpose. Today, as never before, we crave a *sense of pattern*. Today, as never before, the world scatters our inner force in all directions and threatens to turn us into automatons, zombies, or gibbering idiots. Today, as never before, we are compelled to rely on our own sense of destiny. No longer led by tradition, we must follow our own path by the light of our own consciousness and interior wisdom.

Although the work of Freud, Spock, and Piaget forms a fairly comprehensive picture of the developmental patterns of childhood and adolescence, research has tended to ignore the adult life cycle. But attitudes can change quickly, especially in the United States. The pressing need to chart and decode the life rhythms of adults has recently produced a whole crop of lifecycle scholars.

This book does not attempt to present a philosophical speculation of the nature of time; it is largely a preliminary survey of a few of the basic life rhythms to be found in biography. But any serious discussion of human existence in time inevitably raises the question of the full measure of human nature. Empiricism, graphs, and statistics only skim the surface, so we must face the fact that we also need to examine biography from an *esoteric* point of view. After all, we are more than the sum total of events and experiences which comprise our biography. It must be understood, therefore, that much of the inspiration behind this book has come from the light Rudolf Steiner has thrown on the spiritual dimension of human destiny.

Steiner's life and works remain as an irradiating inspiration which enlivens minds and hearts and brings wills to bear on the crucial problems and dilemmas facing modern life. He devoted his considerable inner resources to reminding humankind of its spiritual origin and its immense creative potential for new consciousness and social achievement. He worked to mobilize and encourage the powers of human perception and thinking and integrate them with the devotional, moral-spiritual development of the individual. This, he urged, would enable human consciousness to tackle the pressing problems in art, science, education, economy, medicine, farming, and politics wrought by a pervasive materialism. His Anthroposophy is the foundation for a fresh expansion of knowledge, consciousness, and the new social forms which will arise out of them. Rudolf Steiner's insight into human destiny and the historical process time and time again renewed and encouraged my own stumbling efforts to unravel some of the mysteries within biography.

Attentively watching my life's courses over three decades, charting its transitions, blockages, and accelerations, I began to uncover the ties between my befores and my afters, sowings and reapings, pauses and surges. But more, this change in my attitude to time enabled me to forgive the pain of my childhood, since it had unmistakably engineered the ineluctable drive behind all of my life's themes. This book is a meandering expedition through the kingdom of time and may well raise more questions than it answers, but by accepting the invitation to come along, the reader will be given insight to better appreciate the purposeful and authentic continuity of the life span. This can only uphold the commitment to the journey and heighten the feeling for the uniqueness of our own miraculous migration through time. The phenomenon of human existence is incredibly rich in detail and altogether a highly bewildering affair. Looking at the natural rhythmicity of life first, we will then be in a position to consider how the individual organizes experiences into a coherent and meaningful order. In turn, these conclusions will compel us to face some of the deeper, more esoteric problems of human destiny.

This book is written for those making their first appraisal of Rudolf Steiner's insight into the laws behind the human life span. It observes biography from an exoteric position. An esoteric study of the connection between the heart and biography, history, sacred geometry, metrology, and cosmology is in preparation.

1

Rhythms
and
Cycles

"To everything there is a season and a time to every
purpose under the heavens. A time to be born and a
time to die, and a time to plant and a time to pluck up
that which has been planted." —Ecclesiastes 3:1

Biography reminds me of the leaflike dendrites of frost mysteriously appearing on a winter windowpane, exquisite patterns
etched by an invisible hand directed by the laws of form and
time. At birth, our lives stretch out before us on untouched panes
of space and time, but slowly and inevitably our biographies
crystallize into intricate patterns shaped by identifiable laws.

We can take this thought a step further by viewing biography
as a higher octave of biology. In both human and plant life,
"something" expresses itself, "something" emerges into space
and time. Naturally, plant development is confined to alterations in form and function according to the species, but in
humankind we detect the emergence of personality, consciousness, and biographical events. We never see the plant in its
totality at any one moment because it is always becoming or

passing away in a flux of changing forms. Only by capturing, in a single glance, all its moments, all the sequential steps of unfolding, can we visualize its totality—its complete "idea."

Likewise, we capture only fragments of an individual's wholeness by observing gestures, speech, physiognomy, and social responses. To know a person in depth, we must see the structure of experiences and their effect on character and consciousness; we must see the person's movement through time. Only by viewing the individual as a *time-being* can we decipher the "story" and sense the real center of a personality striving to add to the sum total of itself by attracting new experience.

To pierce the veil of appearances we must first acknowledge the individual as a traveler in time. We soon realize that time endows a person with far more reality than is evident in any single moment. The view of a river seen close up alters considerably when we look at it from a distance. Then we can marvel at the majestic contours shaped by the thrust which carved its path to the sea. Similarly, we may not fathom or warm to a person who at a particular moment of time is blundering forward, attracting disaster at every turn. But a look at the broad tableau of a person's life discloses something of the tortuous saga of becoming. This long view of events and the changing self awareness of the individual is far more real than the present appearance and predicament. We reach a deeper level of communication; we come a little closer to the irreducible core of who the person is. A full biographical view would recognize the germination of skills and talents, not to mention the dysfunctions of the formative years which cause imbalance. These dysfunctions pursue a person through time and create one crisis after another until faced and overcome. All this is nothing less than self-genesis. As a person ages, so a person is born. Both birth and death are present in every moment. Every biographical detail is part of the whole. Every experience is a tributary flowing into the mainstream of purpose and direction. This kind of recognition, this "personology," is far superior to and more supportive than one based on momentary opinions, feelings, and mere facts. Just compare this approach to the one demonstrated ad nauseam in recent years. Time and time again, our great personalities, the hills from whence cometh our help, have been broken into rubble, leveled by myopic critics who peer into every nook and cranny with their reductive minds. But reducing great souls to insignificant, commonplace fragments to titillate our interest in the ambiguities of their sex lives, whims, and fancies obscures their true dimensions and the glorious continuity of their destinies.

The Time Organism

All life emerges and evolves step by step, phase by phase, through a succession of forms from elementary to more complex stages of existence. The elements and energies of the primeval chaos could never have combined to follow various lines of development unless there was some design or order. Every organism must in some way arrange its activities in an order according to its portion of time. In this book, I shall use the term "time organism" to represent the active organizing principle responsible for regulating the cyclic behavior found in every dynamic process, from the mitotic minuet of the amoeba to the changing states of human consciousness. Not only does this time organism orchestrate the biological activity in cells and humans, it must also relate it to the environment. No particle of life is an end unto itself; its biological activity must be properly synchronized to the cycles of every other particle making up the whole organism. Any breakdown in the time mesh tends to throw the organism back into chaos.

Rhythm without time is inconceivable. Rhythm is the particular quality of time which regulates an organism's passive and active phases, inhalation and exhalation, contraction and expansion, growth and reproduction, life and death. Only through its innate rhythms can a living thing absorb matter and energy from its environment and give something of itself in return; only through rhythm can it adjust its interior life to the life outside. Thus, every life process depends on the rhythmic rapport between its inner and outer worlds. A living thing functions and develops because it is immersed in the rhythmic tension produced by two or more fields of energy. On a cosmic scale, it would appear that the universe is able to slough off its old forms and states to create new ones because the cosmos itself is one huge time organism. Even the inorganic world is not really dead if we consider the earth immersed in a living, breathing cosmos. For example, the formation of rocks and their breakdown and reconstitution is rhythmic, as are the ponderous upthrust of continents and their submergence into the sea. Rhythm also regulates the aeons of heat and ice and sustains the earth's crucial rapport with its envelopes of water, air, warmth, and vegetation.

Expansion and contraction is a key motif in this book. Plant life, for example, uses this elementary principle to lift itself to fruition. Perhaps we can imagine the "idea," the invisible design of the plant, unfolding its forms and functions through rhythms of increase and decrease. Plants can manifest themselves in passing time only because they obey the laws of their cycles. To make this point clearer, let us look briefly at the process expressing itself through cycles of vegetative and reproductive activity. Various expansions of growth and contractions of form follow a sequence which culminates in the supreme contraction of the seed. The leaf represents one expansion, while flowering is a contraction producing the diminutive organs of fertilization. The next phase is the expansion of the fruit, followed by a final contraction which impresses the idea of the species into a tiny speck of super matter ready for its return to the earth. Thus birth leads to death, but the idea is passed on to the next generation. Chromosomes and genes may be said to bear the imprint of the plant's memory (it must remember what species it belongs to), but its time principle controls the *timing*, the spacing of the transformations. The plant also belongs to a greater whole—it is delicately suspended between the earth and the sun, and its internal clocks must be synchronized to the rhythms of both its earthly and its cosmic environment.

Expansion and contraction is easier to identify in the miraculous transformation of insect life. But this incredible process is also dependent on a time organism synchronized to certain external rhythms such as the circadian (daily) cycle. The insect's idea, like the plant's, is omnipresent, although the form and structure of the creature alters beyond all recognition.

Take for example, the butterfly. The seedlike egg represents the supreme contraction that "expands" into the caterpillar. This phase is followed by a contraction—the formation of a cocoon. The emergent butterfly is the elegant expansion; its ephemeral beauty lasts just long enough for it to find a safe place for its eggs, thus closing the cycle.

EGG LARVA PUPA BUTTERFLY EGG

Contraction—Expansion—Contraction—Expansion—Contraction

Immobility—-Mobility—Immobility—-Mobility—-Immobility

Biological Clocks

Increasing attention has recently been drawn to the presence of rhythms and cycles in every kind of phenomenon. This remarkable surge of interest has overthrown the blinkered view of living things as isolated or closed systems, whether they be simple cells or human communities. In addition, the new ecological awareness has compelled us to look at our planet as a unified organism in which all hierarchies of life are interdependent. The threatened collapse of certain natural chains of organic life necessary for our survival has shocked us into an almost desperate appreciation for the unity of life.

Research has demonstrated that the intricate time structures in nature control the amazing synchrony between a creature's internal life processes and the world external to it. All living things use their innate time sense to integrate themselves with their surroundings. The simple cell, for example, can be thought of as a biological clock synchronized to legions of sister cells; every member of a cell community is connected to and harmoniously synchronized with the overall time structure of the whole organism. This biological allegiance to the parent body means that the metabolism of each cell must be strictly regulated. Disrupting this time order results in chaos or anarchy. All the complicated cycles of temperature, acidity, hormone activity, immunity, etc., must be tightly attuned if the organism is to preserve its biological balance and health.

But more, every creature is a clock within a clock. According to Michel Gaugelin in his book *Cosmic Clocks,* such biological clocks exhibit incomprehensible variations while under strictly controlled laboratory conditions. When deprived of their normal cycles, plants and animals reveal the hitherto unnoticed presence of certain cosmic rhythms. They respond to subtle changes taking place in the geophysical environment.

A plant, for example, displays an astonishing variety of rhythms and cycles by day and by night. The meticulous tempo of the dance of the flower controls the rise and fall of its leaves, and the gyrations of flowers, tendrils, shoots, and root-tips, in addition to the internal cycles of cell division, rest, photosynthesis, flowering, and reproduction. The time organism choreographs leaf movements, sap circulation, opening and closing of the flower chalice, and the phases of transformation culminating in the seed. Furthermore, the plant adapts its tempo to seasonal alterations in the ratio of daylight and darkness which trigger the change from vegetative to reproductive phases of activity. When kept in total darkness, however, the plant reverts to a fundamental cycle of twenty-four hours—the circadian cycle. As every real gardener knows, a plant's chronometer prompts it to flower at a particular time of the day, night, or year; this yearly cycle is called the "circannual" cycle. Obviously, timing is essential for survival. Take the common fruit fly *drosophila*, which must reach adulthood about an hour before dawn. The timing is crucial since the fly must take advantage of the high relative humidity so that its soft body can expand to its full size and then harden to a waterproof exterior before the dry air of the day can dehydrate it. Similarly, timing is all in the highly organized feeding cycles of the cockroach and the mosquitoes in equatorial Africa that bite during a period of thirty minutes a day. Similarly, the honeybee workers relax in the hive until their favorite flowers are ready with a fresh supply of nectar. As the season advances, they adjust their interior clocks to synchronize with the timing of the blossoming.

Presumably, the intimate companionship between insect and plant kingdoms depends upon the synchrony of their activity cycles. The honeybee, for example, which adapts its cycles of exploration to the flower's readiness for fertilization, soon adjusts its cycles to a new local time after being moved to a distant location. Each insect is also synchronized to the internal clock of its colony in general and its queen in particular. Like the plants, insect and animal time organisms depend on light. The activity cycles of rodents, for example, directly correspond to the rhythm of light and darkness controlling the level of their adrenal hormones.

Marine life flourishing in the zone between high and low tides regulates its metabolism to lunar (tidal) rhythms as well as to the solar cycle of day and night. Mussels, for instance, continue to maintain perfect synchrony to the tidal waters of their origin when moved to still water. Even if taken from the east coast to the west coast of America, they soon reset their clocks to local time. Similarly, the surface camouflage of the fiddler crab lightens and darkens each day according to a twenty-four-hour solar cycle, while its behavior cycle matches the lunar day of 24.8 hours.

So every kind of animal has a personal clock to regulate its life cycles. These timers run with remarkable accuracy for days and weeks, even when the animal is removed from its natural habitat and confined to the controlled climate of a laboratory. Even more startling is the fact that animals continue to respond to circadian rhythms despite the removal of all sorts of organs. Dr. E. Bunning removed a section of a hamster's intestine and found that the removed intestine continued to show its characteristic circadian contractions for three days!

Plant, insect, and animal clocks are also attuned to the time organism of the earth and cosmos, and naturally so, because all living things are immersed in the geophysical force fields of the environment. Dr. F. Brown, of Northwestern University, found that worms and mud snails are sensitive not only to the rhythmic fluctuations of the earth's magnetic and electrostatic field, but also respond to the subtle rhythms of cosmic radiation.

The yearly or circannual rhythm is especially important in the struggle for survival. Some vertebrates hibernate in periods when the rigors of winter and scarcity of food threaten their survival. Survival is enhanced if all members of a particular species have synchronized activity cycles. Not only do the sexes have a better chance of mating, but the presence of large numbers of prey at a given time should be sufficient to satiate the appetites of predators without decimating the prey population. This means that the rhythms of carnivorous creatures must be synchronized to the activity rhythms of their prey. Similarly, the rhythms of parasitic animals are synchronized to their hosts. The microorganisms responsible for malaria, elephantiasis, and other insect-transmitted diseases circulate in the blood and are most infectious at night when certain insects are most active. Accumulating evidence suggests that the grand order, economy, and unity of nature is maintained by a time wisdom which expresses itself in the amazing interplay of countless rhythms and cycles. This time wisdom triggers the elver's journey from the Sargasso Sea and the old eel's return; it prompts the migrant swallow to take wing to Africa, and, as we shall see later on, plays its mysterious role in the genesis of human biography.

The Role of Rhythm

There are many signs that modern medicine is beginning to retrieve, in a new form, the ancient knowledge that every organ in the human body belongs to an all-encompassing unity. Our life depends on a microuniverse of interlocked cycles, every organ held in a rhythmic tension by a staggering number of cycles within cycles. If a particular body rhythm becomes unmeshed or desynchronized, the irregularity disturbs the other cycles. Abnormal rhythms have been discovered in a wide range of illnesses. But, even more important, any distortion in the time order of our organic functions eventually affects our psychological balance. Thus, helping the body resynchronize its errant rhythms is one of the most basic tasks of medicine. The circadian cycle seems to be the fundamental metronome regulating our physical life, and all the shorter rhythms such as pulse and breath, and the longer monthly and yearly cycles seem to be attuned to it. Not only does the circadian throb regulate excretions of liver, kidneys, pancreas, etc., it also governs the tides of antibodies responsible for our immunity to infection and even our mental alertness and sensitivity to taste, smell, and sound. The circulatory system is the fundamental carrier of our innate rhythmicity. When a rhythm becomes retarded or accelerated, the whole organism has to compensate. Naturally, failure to adjust leads to imbalance and sickness. When certain cells, for example, divorce themselves from the natural time order of the body, they are said to be malignant. In this sense, cancer is a time aberration. When our biorhythms are harmonious, we notice little except perhaps a feeling of well-being, but any deviation from the natural frequencies will sooner or later warn us of impending breakdown.

All of us are circadian beings by nature. But everyone's body chemistry is unique. This is why one person is alert and active during certain hours, while another feels tired and listless. Obviously, our daily life would be far more productive and less exhausting if we coordinated our activities to our personal rhythms. Even during our hours of slumber the brain is full of rhythmic activity. Our brain waves reflect the definite electro-chemical differences between awakeness, dreaming, and deep sleep as we pass through several levels of consciousness in a single night.

Our organic rhythms also determine our vulnerability to allergies, toxins, and infections, and our response to medication. Organ transplants in particular have made doctors far more aware of the need for meticulous timing in the application of drugs. There is now no doubt that cycles determine the effectiveness of drugs and the body's resistance to side effects.

Of course, we cannot separate our psychological life from the physical organs which make it possible. Gay Gaer Luce's books on biological rhythms are essential reading for anyone interested in the incredible range and significance of biorhythms. Not only does she provide a detailed survey of rhythm in almost every aspect of biological phenomena, she also includes abundant proof of the connection between organic rhythms and behavior. Research has shown that emotional pressures, travel, isolation, and even work schedules can upset the natural time-order of our metabolic, respiratory, glandular, and sleep cycles. Any serious disturbances in the time organism eventually produce psychological stress, fluctuations in growth, or physical or mental illness. This is why abnormal rhythms have been found in patients suffering from such ailments as migraine, asthma, anxiety neurosis, manic depression, and memory aberrations.

Recent research has discovered that our personal time organism also is influenced by the circadian and noncircadian rhythms of our environment such as barometric pressure, ionization, magnetic fields, and lunar and cosmic rhythms! Furthermore, lunar rhythms have been detected in certain patterns of crime, psychosis, kleptomania, road accidents, suicide rates, and several forms of mental disturbance.

In this chapter, I briefly survey some of the findings of orthodox science pertaining to the various time phenomena of nature and humankind. But I would also strongly urge the reader to examine the research of Rudolf Steiner in this field. His spiritual inquiry into the function of the time organism stresses its regulatory effect on the biological cycles of plant, animal, and human, not to mention its role in the dynamics of the human psyche and spirit. For a start, I would recommend a study of the comprehensive work by Guenther Wachsmuth, *The Etheric Formative Forces in Cosmos, Earth and Man.* Also to be recommended are the educational books by Rudolf Steiner which examine the working of the individual time organism responsible for the phases of growth and consciousness underlying child development.

We dwell in time and unfold our physical and biographical evolution within it. To do this, we must, according to Steiner, possess an individual time organism, a "time body" which is closely integrated with the physical body on the one hand and with the cyclic life of the cosmos on the other. To exist within time we need more than a physical organism. We also need another kind of body, a "life body" which is organized according to the laws of time and permits every individual to unfold a life in processional time. In sharp contrast to the gravitational forces, this "time body" is both fashioned and maintained by the upbuilding, formative, integrating forces that elevate dead inorganic matter into life-filled organic realms. These forces are contained in an energy system which monitors, sustains, and governs the rhythmicity and the developmental patterns in human life.

The spectrum of rhythm covers every aspect of human life. Besides the more obvious cycles of illness, etc., cycles of longer duration have been found in church membership, marriage and death rates, economic fluctuations, production levels, the stock market, and war. Graphs show the strange correspondence between social phenomena and sunspot cycles, lunar rhythms, and periodic changes in cosmic radiation. Cycles have been discovered in everything from the population density of red squirrels and salmon to the world production of lead and patterns of heart disease. Rhythm, then, directs the ebb and flow of our organic life, but it also sustains the higher faculties of our nature. In fact one could say that most of the mental disorder in both individuals and societies stems from a serious lack of rhythm. The bewildering hurly-burly of life, the pressure imposed by forces outside ourselves, ever threaten to smother our natural cycles. We have lost our natural sense of rhythm, our sense of timing. We do not know when to ebb and when to flow!

A rhythm-poor lifestyle makes us displaced and disabled persons. How then can we better sense and strengthen the rhythmic order of life? How can we best filter, absorb, and digest the experiences which tend to overwhelm us? Every person has his or her own time dynamic. There are particular times of the day, month, year, and life span when we are more creative and energetic, while at other times we struggle against lethargy. If we could but shape our life according to our innate rhythms, we would certainly be more at ease with ourselves.

It is a matter of digestion. Every organism must digest everything it receives properly, rhythmically. What is true for the biological world is also true for the psychological. Our anxieties, emotions, sense impressions, griefs, and sorrows, have to be *properly digested*. If the pressure of undigested experience overwhelms the system, our biorhythms slip out of gear. Likewise, the major experiences and crises which comprise our biography must be adequately digested before they can unite with the core of our being. Only when the psyche has digested the "nutritional" experiences which come to it can a fresh cycle of impulses trigger a new phase of action. Any imbalance in the digestive process, whether physiological or psychological, will eventually unleash the energies which produce the crisis needed to restore the equilibrium.

The same is true for society. Society has to digest the achievements of its scientific and political thinking as well as the results of its social and economic actions. Without feeling, without art, craft, drama, literature, music, and religion, society becomes imbalanced to the point of schizophrenia. Only through its moral-feeling-aesthetic faculties can society develop sensitivity enough to judge any destructive ideas it comes up with and prevent them from being pressed into action. A balanced culture depends on rhythmic communication between itself and the individual, between the national psyche and the individual psyche. Rhythmic societies continually heal themselves. The early cultures were upheld by their rhythmic rituals. Unrhythmic, desensitized, artless, irreligious, and polarized cultures suffer from seizures of rebellion and breakdown because individual and community become unmeshed. Many cultures suffer from bouts of social indigestion because, like individuals, nations must properly digest their experiences—especially their disasters!

Synchronicity—"The Sympathy of All Things"

"Synchronicity can become a master key for opening the door to teachings regarding the nature of human destiny that have heretofore been closed to us."

—Carl Jung

We cannot understand the multiverse of rhythms and cycles without considering their interaction—their synchronicity. Earlier on, I presented the thought that the time-organism monitors and regulates the organic activity of the body through a multiplicity of rhythms and cycles. These rhythms are the sutures, so to speak, binding all the functional parts of the body together. But all our rhythms must be synchronized if we are to stay mentally and physically healthy. The "local time" of a single liver cell, for example, must be synchronized to the overall time system of the individual. But now we must ask does the skin mark the boundary of our time organism or "time body"? Is our personal time detached from the all-embracing time order of the earth and cosmos? Are the countless hubs of life on this planet (and even beyond) also synchronized with one another in some way? If the time organism is indeed responsible for the sequential patterns in our life story, is it also synchronized to the time systems of the people who cross our path? Our lives are molded to some extent by the conflicts and crises of our society and nation, and even by the gradual global shifts in consciousness. So ultimately, it would seem possible that everything in our universe may be synchronized to some all-pervading and inscrutable cosmic clock!

Synchronicity offers us a fresh and exciting way of looking at biography. There is a correspondence between oneself and other selves, between self and event, and even between self and the various cosmic rhythms. If something intangible, something we are unconscious of, does shape the pattern of events, then we *have* to question our conventional notions about chance and freedom. Like it or not, synchronicity implies that some events are arranged by forces outside our normal awareness. There are times when events can happen and certain times when they cannot. Such a possibility compels us to take a closer look at *coincidence*. Is there a wisdom, a deeper meaning present when the life of one person "accidentally" intersects the life of another? Such "chance" encounters are important because they shape our lives. They provide all sorts of vital experience—be it guidance, knowledge, support, love, suffering, or disaster.

Take for example, if I were to sleepwalk my way into a lecture audience through boredom, duty, or curiosity, but then hear something which sets my soul afire. It may be a thunderbolt of enlightenment or a gently gnawing idea, but my heart and mind are moved to take a new direction and life can never be the same again. It is a "chance" moment of recognition—"Just what I have been waiting for!"—which alters my life and gives it the fresh momentum of a new dimension. Some dormant seed within was touched by a timely ray from without. Arthur Koestler, for one, would not call it chance. "I have always believed that in the administration of Divine Providence there is a special department entirely concerned with seeing that the right book comes into the hands of a reader at the right moment." [1]

Our hidden sense of timing appears to be infinitely wiser than our waking mind. We see this when the inner self overrules the outer self, as when our best prepared plans and itineraries go

---

1. George Feifer, "Guru of the Western World," *The Daily Telegraph,* No. 562 (September, 1975).

awry, disrupted by an "accident" which later brings great benefit into our life. This "time magnet" drawing self and event together in the name of experience and destiny must be hidden deep in the unconscious depths of the psyche, bringing us experiences when the psyche needs them, whether the mind welcomes them or not. Emerson had a point when he said that one of the primal secrets of the world is the tie between person and event, and that the energy we expend trying to escape our destiny only serves to drive us deeper into it.

Originally coined by Carl Gustav Jung, "synchronicity" refers to "the simultaneous occurrence of two meaningful but not causally connected events." Put simply, coincidence is more than mere chance. Jung suggested that synchronicity is an active element in our psychic life. In *Synchronicity: an Accusal Connecting Principle*, he presents his view that synchronicity is no more mysterious than the strange discontinuities of physics. It is only our deeply entrenched belief in the laws of cause and effect which prevents us from seeing that meaningful coincidence may well be orchestrated by the laws of time which connect person and event. No matter what the probabilities, we tend to ignore meaningful coincidence and chance if we cannot explain it. We leave it in the realm of the unthinkable.

Readers wishing to pursue the idea of synchronicity further should not miss Koestler's brilliant scientific examination of it in *The Roots of Coincidence*. This principle can throw light on biography if it can help us understand the connections between one person's time organism and another's, and the magical interplay of their rhythms and cycles. I believe that Jung was right when he saw synchronicity as a higher law superimposed on the physical laws of action and reaction, cause and effect. It seems to me that our lives unfold according to two sets of laws, two rhythmically meshing planes. One is the world of space and time in which we move and appear to make decisions; the other is a psychic or spiritual world with its own laws. Synchronicity orchestrates the unconscious impulses of our will which lead us to the right place at the right time to meet the event which will change us. Our minds cannot understand it fully, but at least we can look for it in biography.

To sum up the synchrony which connects person to person and person to events endows biography with an added dimension of meaning. A superficial view of life suggests that the world is populated by innumerable hubs of consciousness imprisoned in separate bodies, each battling against the barrage of human experience, straining to fulfill its life as best it can. But we can begin to dispel the loneliness and futility of this strength-sapping illusion by sensing the spiritual-psychic ligaments connecting our personal life to the lives of others. Thus, wherever we look, we see destiny and experience being born, shaped, and fulfilled according to the infinitely wise laws of time. Moreover, if synchronicity is one of the great creative laws of our universe, our humble story becomes an integral part of the biography of humankind and of the very universe.

I believe the principle of synchronicity, though barely understood as yet, reaches its highest expression as the creative element in the formation of biography. Any attempt to unravel the riddles of human destiny has to examine the mysterious rapport that exists between the individual psyche and the world. It is this rapport that gives form, content, and meaning to life. Synchronicity will remind us, though in modern terms, of the ancient's sense of belonging to the unity of the universe. It will show us that each one of us is immersed in an all-encompassing psychic field or continuum and that biography is fashioned by countless interactions in that field—acts of creation in time. Thus synchronicity, the principle of timing, resides in the very meaning of our personal existence. We are never isolated from the ever-changing psychic network, or "mind at large," to use Huxley's phrase. Although our general consciousness is ignorant of it, our unconscious self is not; it is part of the innate wisdom which arranges our possibilities for us. What we do with them is a matter of freedom.

Human and Cosmic Breathing

"Then the Lord God formed man from the dust of the ground and breathed into his nostrils the breath of life." —Genesis 2:7

The notion that our personal time life is contained within the time matrix of the cosmos is an ancient one. The wisdom of antiquity concealed within mythology shows that our ancestors were aware of some of the nonrational aspects of life. Indeed, the imagery and perception behind myths and legends picture the human being as the child of cosmic life. Myths show us that the human mind once experienced life and its cycles as an integral part of the cosmic clock. If the individual is a microcosm, we should be able to detect a numerical correspondence between our personal rhythms and the cosmic cycles. Not only was the old cosmology or star wisdom aware of the time connections between individual and cosmos, but there is also plenty of evidence to support the claim that our ancestors founded their number systems and metrology on this knowledge.

Breathing is the archetype of all cycles. Respiration is a universal principle found in all life no matter what the complexity or line of evolution. Breathing enables the outside to meet the inside and vice versa, so every organism absorbs something from its environment and gives something in return. Not only do we inhale the life-sustaining air and exhale its residues, we also inhale nutritional matter and exhale energy; we inhale sensory information and exhale action; we inhale experience and exhale biography; we inhale at birth and exhale at death.

Even the earth can be said to breathe. Research increasingly confirms that the rhythmic rapport among the earth's geological, watery, gaseous, and biological envelopes is finely tuned to solar and lunar rhythms. But does the cosmos breathe? The Magi of ancient Persia recognized in the encircling dance of planets and stars the rhythmic pulse of a dynamic and meaningful cosmos. Their formidable insight confirmed the earlier belief that the cosmos made humankind in its image. In other words, cosmic rhythms regulate everything from the passage of world ages and the ebb and flow of civilizations to the biographical cycles of the individual. It is a magnificent conception—unity in diversity.

Were the ancients aware of the numerical correspondence between breathing and cosmic cycles? This subject would need a volume for itself; all I wish to do here is highlight the idea of the synchrony between the human time organism and the cosmic clock. Let us take as our base the average number of heart beats and breaths per minute. In one minute, we breathe on average eighteen times, while our heart beats seventy-two times. Now let us take a quantum leap to the cosmic equinoxes. (See diagram 1 on the following page.) Putting it as simply as possible, a star rising at a particular spot on the horizon at seven o'clock on September 29, 1976, will not rise at exactly the same place at the same time on September 29, 1977. The star, together with the whole celestial sphere, appears to creep westward year after year, century after century, until, after nearly 25,920 years, it returns to its earlier position. This cycle, known to the ancients as the "Sacred Year" or "Great Year," means that the zodiac drifts one degree (or gains one day) every seventy-two years. Dividing the Great Year into Great Months gives us a subcycle of 2,160 years, known as the zodiacal epoch (such as the Age of Aquarius, etc.). According to ancient and modern occultism, this "Great Month" represents the cyclic rise and fall of great civilizations.

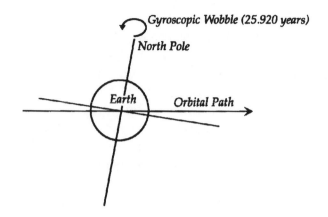

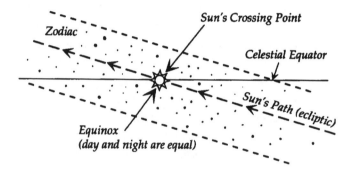

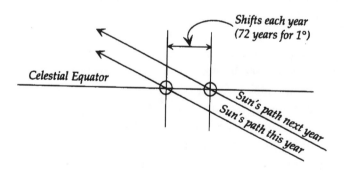

Diagram 1

So we have four significant numbers: a pulse of seventy-two, a breathing cycle of eighteen, a precessional rhythm of 25,920, and a cultural epoch of 2,160. A few simple calculations will disclose several startling correspondences between these numbers. For example, a breathing rate of eighteen per minute means that we breathe 25,920 times in a day, suggesting that our human day is a microcosmic reflection of the Great Year. According to several ancient texts, the prototypical human life span is seventy-two years, which is just three months over 26,000 days. Furthermore, our pulse rate of seventy-two beats per minute is also reflected in the precessional movements of the vernal sun, which moves one degree every seventy-two years. These figures, of course, are approximate, or rather, archetypal. Although based on ancient knowledge, they are reasonably close to modern estimates, despite subtle changes in the earth's rate of rotation and orbit around the sun. There are, moreover, many more such cosmic correspondences between our respiration and the lunar, planetary, and zodiacal clocks, but more than a brief survey would take us beyond the task of this chapter. We should not, however, neglect the cycles of Saturn and Jupiter in biography.

Saturn and its resplendent rings take nearly thirty years (twenty-nine years and one hundred sixty-eight days) to orbit the sun, which means that it makes seventy-two revolutions in a Great Month, passing through 25,920 degrees of the zodiac. Therefore, Saturn is also numerically linked to human respiration, the life span, the Great Month and the Great Year. But what about Jupiter, which circumnavigates the sun once every twelve years? Jupiter orbits the sun 2,160 times in a Great Year, passing through 25,920 signs of the zodiac (one sign per year). Jupiter's cycle in hours is reasonably close to the number of heart beats per day (103,680). Likewise, there are 4,320 heartbeats per hour, nearly the same as the number of days in Jupiter's cycle. So, like Saturn's, the movements of old Jove appear related to the pulse, breath, the Great Month, and the Great Year.

The reader might well argue that by juggling a few basic numbers and their multiples, we can come up with anything. Quite true, but the fact remains, the more we delve into these correspondences, the more we sense the connection between geometry, temple building, cosmology, astronomy, metrology, gematria, and biography. The point of all these numbers and cycles is to suggest that there are connections between the human being's physical cycles and those of the cosmos. If our physical life is so attuned to cosmic cycles, we should not be surprised to find evidence that our spiritual and mental development is too.

The Qualities of Time

"Time enfoldeth and unfoldeth succession."
—Nicholas of Cusa

Time is the crucial element in all rhythm and synchrony, but its role in the design and construction of all biography is highly mysterious. Time has become everyone's religion. It vexes, cheats, mystifies, challenges, ignores, horrifies, and anticipates us. We are immersed in it and it lives in us. Although some seek to kill it, all of us will die because of it. While it carries us away from our pain, it drives us into unforeseen storms. Time gives us space for longing and hope; it also forecloses space and limits hope. It is the inevitable and immutable element in our becoming and passing away. The scientist measures it; the novelist dramatizes it; the sculptor freezes it; the investor speculates with it; the politician prays to it, and historians remember it. Vanity fights it and athletes never outrun it; wisdom is blessed by it—but who understands it?

At least we can safely examine the way time has been measured. In a sense, the clocks invented by humankind reflect the historical process of its emerging consciousness. To put it differently, our "descent" from a mythological, prescientific consciousness to a self-centered awareness of the world is mirrored in our methods of gauging the passage of time. Our early ancestors set the rhythm of their existence to the cycles of the sun, which was both the source of life and the timer of their rituals. The highly ritualized calendric life of individual, tribe, and nation was strictly synchronized to the cosmic cycles by the priest initiates. The sundial with its religious-symbolic meaning of light and shadow was superseded by the Babylonian waterclock. After this came the ingenious and exquisitely handcrafted mechanical clock, which evolved from an increasing preoccupation with the physical world; only an awareness of gravity could have invented the pendulum. Now, the incredibly accurate chronometers of modern science are synchronized to the unerring pulsation of energy within the atom. So we have passed from light to water, to earth, to atomic matter; we have descended from the luminous "time heart" of the cosmos to the invisible rhythmic energy imbedded in the very heart of matter.

Observing the development of our sense of time from childhood to maturity offers us one way of recognizing the different qualities of time. Take the embryo for example; a number of fetal rhythms have been found which suggest that the embryo's biorhythms are synchronized to the mother's circadian rhythms, particularly her sleep cycles. Not only does the fetus sense the rhythmic pulse of the mother's heart and blood vessels, even after birth the baby's activity rhythms are connected to its mother's cycles; indeed the compatibility between mother and baby is largely dependent on her biological, emotional, and sleep cycles. Her child responds not only to her body rhythms but also to her emotional state, her psychic condition. Only in infanthood does the child develop its own distinct circadian patterns; only then will the intermeshed time organisms of mother and child become detached and independent.

Although aware of movements, sounds, and images, the selfless, undifferentiated consciousness of a very young child cannot sever itself from the external world. It is as if the biological universe of embryo and womb changes into the symbiotic union of child and environment. We should realize, moreover, that the baby's sense of time is qualitatively very different from that of its parents, who are dominated by a one-thing-after-another time, a rectilinear time. Perhaps we could say that the baby is cosmically cocooned in an "all-at-once-time," a universal or paradisal time, as were Adam and Eve when they knew not death. Mircea Eliade, in *Myth and Reality*, notes that Freud recognized the significant role of the paradisal time of earliest childhood, the bliss before the break (weaning), that is, before time becomes, for each individual a "living time."

Inevitably the young child takes leave of its paradisal bliss when it becomes aware of another quality of time. It gradually discovers the *cyclic* order of its surroundings, the recurring patterns of day and night, the rituals of dressing, eating, playing, and bedtimes. The infant recognizes the parents' rhythm of leaving for work and anticipates their return. This dreamlike awareness of the repetitious routine of domestic life expands still further to enclose the cyclic return of birthdays, holidays, and festivals. The child, like the primitive, is firmly embedded in the rhythm of the day and the seasons. This wondrous ebb and flow of the cycles arouses the child's senses and feelings, waking on a snowy morn, marveling at the swallows' return, the excitement of sand, sea, and ice cream, scuffling through autumnal carpets. Indeed, the cycles of day and year support the seven-year-old and give him or her a sense of security. Perceptive teachers notice the difference between children raised in rhythmic homes and those brought up in a chaos of irregular meal and bedtimes. The latter develop a poor sense of linear time later on.

The child's subjective sense of time is quite different from the more or less uniform motion of adult time. It speeds up or slows down, matching the pace of snail or cheetah, according to the degree of boredom or excitement. But sadly, all too soon, our children lose the magic ring of cyclic time and begin, as the fairy tales tell them, their journey through the forest of passing time. Their emerging self-consciousness begins to estimate and organize the passage of events. Twelve-year olds begin to appreciate the pageant of history and biography as a time process, and their sense of passing time gives them access to the laws of cause and effect found in subjects like physics and mechanics. Between conception and adolescence, our consciousness emerges from the paradisal to meet the cyclic and finally the linear experience of time. By puberty we should be psychologically adjusted to the passing time in which we find our independence.

Of course, our concept of time depends on our relationship to it, our awareness of it. Like the infant, our ancestors had vastly different feelings about time. Moreover, it is possible to detect in the movements of prehistory and history the advance from a paradisal to a cyclic and then to a linear experience of time. Although history has led us through these different qualities of time, they continue to exist somewhere in the subliminal levels of our being. The movement of our waking mind through time gives us the experience of one-thing-after-another time, while cyclic time vibrates in the magical, semiconscious world of our dreams. Perhaps somewhere in the unconscious depths of the psyche we may find the all-at-once time of eternity—duration without time.

The destiny of humankind and universe, as understood by the ancients, is synchronized to the endless cosmic rhythms rippling across the fields of eternity. Their prelogical awareness was enveloped in the cycles of birth, death, and rebirth imposed by the gods. The ancient Hindus, for example, saw themselves trapped in an endless succession of earth lives until they could achieve perfection and rejoin the primordial time of Nirvana.

The life of early civilizations was intimately connected to the festivals and rituals of their religions, which reminded the people that they dare not ignore their origin in the Great Time. Ritual, myth, initiation rites, and codes of conduct were designed to allow them to *reenter* the Great Time and reconnect themselves to a reality far greater than that experienced by the waking mind. J.B. Priestley, who was himself much preoccupied with the mysteries of time, viewed the Great Time as belonging to the myth, gods, and magical beings of creation. Priestley believed that when primitive people were involved in ceremonial activities, when they relived aspects of the life of their mythological hero, they entered and experienced the all-embracing Great Time: "[Their] world was sustained not by the meaningless passage from dawn to noon to sunset, but by this Great Time, in which all creation, power, and magic, existed."[2] The purpose of ritual was to produce a particular state of mind in the participants, who were thereby freed from the prison of the profane world and entered the Sacred Time. Their consciousness thrown open to the spirit of a creative, life-filled cosmos, they were then resanctified and regenerated by immersion in the all-at-once time. Ritual life also meant that gods and their mortal representatives guided the destiny of the individuals through their crises and transformations.

Myths were more than recordings of the labors of the gods; they were a means of re-creating the gods' dominion over the present. The myth gave human beings access to their sacred history, and its powerful symbols touched the deepest levels of their souls. The ritual, which really reenacted the past, guided

---

2. J.B. Priestley, *Man and Time*, Laurel edition. (New York: Dell Publishing Company, 1968)

the destinies of individuals and renewed their kinship with humanity, nature, and cosmos.

In mythology, the closed ring of cyclic time is perfectly pictured as the serpent—the "ouroboros." Embracing the sphere of eternity, this cosmic serpent swallows its own tail and sloughs off its skins of life and death. In Norse myths, the Midgard serpent encircled the world of humans until the cataclysmic end of the cosmic age when Thor and serpent destroyed each other in violent combat. Thus the hammer blows of Thor broke the old, circular, serpent time which had dominated the early pre-ego consciousness of humanity. The closed cycle became the *arrow* of passing time. Armed with self-will and his own mind, the hero could now make his way into history in search of himself.

Humanity's inexorable drive toward self-consciousness (what Jung called "individuation") meant that the cyclic view of time became obscured by the preoccupation with chronological time. We have already noted the Chaldean's interest in measuring the movements of planets and stars, and the Greek mind went further. As the veils of the provisional world covered the sacred mysteries of Greece, humans became more and more involved with their senses and in the search for natural laws. Obviously, there can be no science of cause and effect without a sense of passing time. The gain of consciousness in Greece silenced the oracles and barred humans from the Great Time of their ancestors. By losing sight of the cyclic order of birth, death, and rebirth, the Greeks realized they were fastened to the chain of passing time, which dragged them from the cradle to the grave. Withdrawing from atavistic awareness, the Hellenes sensed death's tragic interruption of their existence. To compensate for this loss, the old temple rituals were transformed into the art forms of *tragedy*, but the aims were the same: to break through the temporal consciousness of the audience—to break through passing time. Tragedy, like ritual, alters the focus of the mind; it transmutes and elevates consciousness.

The Romans finally dethroned mythology and cyclic time; the eagle of Rome was earth-bound, trapped in the expanding web of military, judicial, and mercantile life. Although the conflict between the two views of time spluttered on into the Middle Ages, the voice of astrologers and alchemists was drowned by the clamor of science and geographical exploration. Sir Isaac Newton became the foremost champion of linear time when he assumed that absolute time flowed at a uniform rate independently of the world and of human consciousness of it.

Linear time, in the guise of technology, science, and economics now reigns over Western culture. It is a jealous tyrant, ruling by fear, commanding us to worship progress. It tells us to take out insurance policies for a future it will cheat us of. It calls itself "money" and cries, "Grab what you can while you may. You can't take it with you. Buy now, pay later. You only live once." It insists that we have left the bad old days and are on course for a golden future, but in the same breath it announces that we are in full flight for a doomsday of overpopulation or genocide! Unwittingly, we are well and truly bound by the tense hawser of a time which gives us ulcers, high blood pressure, and stiffening joints while we struggle to keep up with its timetables and mortgages. Deaf to our hopes and enemies of patience, our clocks command us in the name of progress to accelerate our rate of change. They insist that we demolish the sanctuaries of tradition, by violence if necessary, to build the future *now*!

It is difficult to think of qualities of time other than the linear variety which has squeezed the vastness of eternity into a thin thread of awareness severed by death. Apparently, all we can experience is a series of now's. The past is dead and we have no proof that the future will arrive. Whatever happened to the all-at-once time, the dimension of time where nothing perishes, where nothing is lost, where *was*, *is*, and *will be* form a glorious unity of experience? Our sterile, soulless view of time has greatly diminished our perception of life. Yes, the arrow of time has wounded the spirit of humanity. The spiritual human being seems to dissolve in this stream of time; only the skeleton feels comfortable in it.

But all is not lost. There are signs of rebellion in every quarter as the shift of modern consciousness slowly undermines the dynasty of passing time. Einstein's attack on Newton's absolute time gave the movement intellectual respectability by suggesting that time is relative. The books of the English airplane designer and philosopher John Dunne, *An Experiment with Time* and *The Serial Universe*, lent impetus to the cause. Playwrights, novelists, and film makers are increasingly probing the time problem, while time travelers of science fiction contort time to put us among the dinosaurs or on the star trails of galactic space. The surge of interest in extrasensory perception and parapsychology has also done much to unmask the deceptions of linear time. All this, together with the Western mind's flirtation with Eastern thought and occultism, points to a new awakening, a renaissance of time. Even our physicists are trying to reverse time.

The conclusion is inescapable. Altering our state of mind changes our awareness of time. Not only is time distorted, retarded, or accelerated by changes in our metabolism or temperature, but our relationship to it alters when we dream or when we face imminent danger and relive our years in seconds. Anesthetics, alcohol, stimulants, and especially the hallucinogenic drugs such as LSD alter our sense of time. We also sense time differently under hypnosis, in deep meditation, and during mental and emotional disturbances. Indeed, a subjective time sense is sometimes used as an indicator in the diagnosis of psychotic and schizophrenic patients. At the highest level, the seer or initiate with all the inner doors of the psyche thrown open experiences a sudden epiphany. In this blessed state, such men as Pascal, Blake, and Jacob Boehme have broken through the time-barrier. This revelation of what has been called "cosmic consciousness" is a move into the all-at-once time of the spirit. Perhaps the march of human consciousness will one day lead everyone into the deepest recesses of his or her being to experience time in its fullness.

The Coil of Biographical Time

When Mother Maria said, "Time is the ship which carries thee, it is not thy home," she was referring to the successional time which rules the brain, permitting us to view only the procession of events passing before our senses. But we can lift our sense of time and timing beyond the restrictive illusions of transitory time by contemplating the possible existence of other dimensions of qualities of time. As we have seen, there is plenty of evidence to support the view that passing time has *no dominion over the processes at work in our soul and spirit.* Cyclic time appears to govern the upper regions of the psyche, while the deepest roots of our personal reality reside in the infinite "forever." I believe, therefore, that we may well exist within a threefold time order where the cyclic aspect of time *mediates* between the linear, waking mind and the all-at-once Great Time. In other words, rhythmic time, the harmonizer, mediator, and coordinator of our physical and spiritual functions, enables the eternal in us to live and grow in the passing time of the mortal world. As this cyclic time regulates the digestion and transformation of our life experience, a study of biographical rhythms should uncover many meaningful patterns.

Perhaps the best way to visualize time is to imagine it as a synthesis of linear time and cyclic time, a three-dimensional spiral. Our emergence into biographical time begins at birth.

This is the moment when we enter the "biographsphere" where experience is prepared for and encountered at the correct place and time, then digested and incorporated into who and what we are. Only by entering rhythmic time can we begin what Laurens van der Post calls our "battle for new being." But we do not campaign alone, we are members of the human community—we share the "time sympathy" of the mesocosm. This is where our personal spiral intercepts the spirals of others, and the mysterious filaments of synchronicity spark the combustion of new experience.

Rhythmic time governs only the *position*, the placement of events, *not what we do with them nor how we react to them.* Appearing like leaves spiraling along our lengthening stem of passing time, every incident, crisis, and change in course has its own proper and meaningful place. Yet each experience is a seed planted in the continuum of rhythmic time to germinate in the right season. Because we retain our past, no experience is futile, infertile, or lost. Out of sight or out of mind, our life experience continues to live within us where it is dealt with by the "juices" of our psychic digestion, our spiritual metabolism.

Thus, those things left undone, the missed opportunities, errors, and misjudgments, continue to prepare future stages for their correction, completion, and redemption. Likewise, our suffering and setbacks serve to release new forces in the psyche which, when the time is ripe, "lead on to fortune." The laws of rhythm decree that all things must take their course. Ideas, ambitions, and decisions have their own good time for implementation, while impatience leads to the failure which should either disperse our illusions or strengthen our convictions. If, on the other hand, we miss the crucial moment for action, the possibility passes and we must await another turn of the spiral.

This meaningful view of a creative time implies that the mysterious encounter between person and event is not a matter of chance. Many scientific discoveries, for example, appear at first sight to be nothing more than an astonishing series of coincidences, but the word chance becomes redundant when we examine the *timing*. Take the case of Sir Alexander Fleming, who dedicated his career to the study of defense mechanisms in the battle against infection. To all outward appearances, his critical decisions and discoveries were based on trivialities and accidents. Fleming chose to open his career at St. Mary's Hospital because of its water-polo team! Furthermore, he was selected to join the laboratory staff of Sir Almoth Wright because his skill as a rifleman would be an asset to their team! Of course the quality of Fleming's mind was a significant factor, but the actual decisions were undoubtedly influenced by something other than medicine. Later, the "chance" drop of a tear, coupled with Fleming's astute perception, triggered his study of the sterilizing power of the lysozyme. Again, the "chance" speck of bacteria settling on an old mold set the stage for his discovery of penicillin. Every link in this chain of discovery had a particular position in passing time; but we must attribute the results to the preparedness of Fleming's mind, which was ready to make something from these flashes of synchronicity. Obviously then, the time element plays a crucial role in the act of creation. Only in the passing time of the intellect do discovery and invention appear to be accidental or sometimes instantaneous. But this is only the surface, the result of a creative process rooted in the deepest regions of the psyche and other dimensions of time.

Let us now consider another aspect of this idea. For example, what happens when a particularly meaningful image makes an unusually deep impression on the emotions? As a child, Albert Schweitzer was deeply moved by a statue of an African, part of a monument by Bertholdi which stands in the town square of Colmar. Whenever he could, Schweitzer went to see this melancholy stone; "His face with its sad expression spoke to me of the misery of the Dark Continent," Schweitzer said. Reinforced by several visits during his student years, the profound and disturbing presence of this image continued to work in the underworld of his soul. Many years later, despite the advice of his friends, Schweitzer felt compelled to alter the course of his career by studying medicine and then serving the African community he established in Lamberene. We might rightly ask if this statue was a part of Schweitzer's destiny; was he meant to see it? Did this provocative image with its frozen cry sink into the substratum of his soul where it was heard and recognized by "something" in the very nucleus of his being? Did this image then generate the impulse which later, according to the law of rhythmic time, returned to the waking mind to influence Schweitzer's decisions?

I believe a meaningful psychology of the life span can be established by studying the time relationships between our early experiences and their consequences later in life. Eventually, perhaps, our awareness of the time order and wisdom of life will lead us to acknowledge the idea that we deliberately seek our experiences, and that biography is synonymous with destiny. This possibility raises several fascinating questions. Does the real kernel of our reality belong to the Great Time where past and future coexist? Or to put it differently, does the unactualized master pattern of our life exist in the Great Time, but only become biography in the provisional world of passing time? Does biography represent our struggle to make happen some preexistent master plan, task, or mission? But we have come too far too soon; these speculations should be set aside for the moment while we examine some of the more obvious biographical rhythms.

Chapter 1 has presented a picture of the human being as a rhythmic being living in the passing time of its becoming, immersed in the rhythmic tides which sweep across the great spaces of the universe. On a personal level, it has suggested that we look for rhythm in everything from the automatic cycles responsible for our physical survival to the psychological digestion of life experience and the unfolding scenario of our life story. It also suggests that our personal time is meshed with the cycles of the world and universe and that there are specific laws governing the time affinities of human relationships. There is a "time sympathy" between person and event.

The next three chapters will present the reader with a specific problem. At first sight, there seems to be little difference among the functional activities of the seven-year, twelve-year, and thirty-year cycles as far as biographical events are concerned. Close examination, however, will prove otherwise. We should recognize in each cycle a typical character, a particular quality, a specific biographical process and emphasis. The seven-year cycle is predominantly a rhythm which regulates long-term alterations of consciousness—one's experience of one's own psyche—although, in many cases, these interior shifts are connected to events and crises triggered by the external world. Similarly, serious study will disclose that the twelve-year cycle is primarily a vocational rhythm, the expression of the psyche in the world of personal action. Lastly, the thirty-year cycle, although bearing many character traits of the other two, marks the great archetypal phases and transition points of life. Many difficulties arise, because these cycles are interconnected; each is integral to the overall spiritual-psychic organism of the individual. Only a patient exploration of biography in both depth and span can identify the uniquely subtle properties of each rhythm.

2

The Sacred Seven

"Time, like a brilliant steed with seven rays, full of fecundity, bears all things onward."
—Artharva Veda XII 53

"The seventh year always transforms man. It brings about a new life, a new character and a different state."
—Martin Luther

A serious examination of this cycle in biography will disclose its connection to the sequence of stages in the ego-self's movement toward a more mature perception of its own existence. In specific terms, it is the rhythm of psychological and spiritual growth, meaning the acquisition and digestion of life experience. It modulates the rapport between the growing mind and the deeper, unconscious levels of our being.

Just a glance at the universal presence of the seven in myth and religion will indicate its sacred quality. The significant seven is sprinkled throughout the Bible—for example, the seven years which Jacob served Leah to win Rachel, the seventy years of bondage, and the seven months the Ark of the

Covenant lay in the land of the Philistines. There is also the sevenfold circuit of Jericho, the sevenfold dream of Pharaoh, and the seven daughters of Jethro. The seven is also conspicuous in the Apocalypse of St. John, just as in Hebrew ritual with its seven altars, seven sacred wells, seven sacred lamps, the seven-branched candlestick, seven planets, and seven levels of Heaven. Likewise, the Hindu religion speaks of the seven Holy Rishis and the seven Sanskrit *Manvantaras* which denote the seven stages in the development of the universe.

We can also recognize the universality of this sacred number in the beings our ancestors knew as the guiding spirits of humanity. They were known as the seven Devas of India, seven Genii of Hermes, seven Amshaspands of Persia, seven Angels of Chaldea, and seven Archangels of the Apocalypse. The key here is that each of these high "intelligences" had a specific mission and time cycle of influence on evolution. The evolution of a microcosmic human is an image of the macrocosmic universe still evolving. It is no wonder the seven appears everywhere.

There is obviously something psychological and spiritual about the seven. For example, the initiates in the ancient Mystery Centers, those custodians of the sacred wisdom found in all the great civilizations, were taught that they could transform and expand their self-awareness through seven thresholds of consciousness. This is why the seven is known as the number of initiation or spiritual development. This mention of initiation may appear to have little in common with the subject of biography, but both initiation and biography involve a pattern of self-development, and both involve the seven. Indeed, our struggle through time is a crude but true form of initiation, inasmuch as it is a journey of self-discovery. It is no coincidence that initiation has seven degrees and that biography has a seven-year cycle. Would-be initiates, under strict surveillance, consciously strive for the supernal heights of consciousness. We, however, are initiated into the lower mysteries of ourselves by that remorseless disciplinarian we call "life experience." But the aims are the same: to make us conscious of our reality and our true relationship to the world and universe. The task of the old Temple Mysteries was to change the disciples' relationship to self and cosmos; the disciples could be reborn and could learn the innermost secrets of their real nature, its origin, meaning, and mission. For us, however, our wise masters are the obstacles we meet as we blunder and limp our way along a path we barely recognize. *Aging* and its subdued heroism change our relationship to ourselves and life. Life commands us to awaken. More often than not, the "slings and arrows of outrageous fortune" are nothing but the ricochet of our own reflected errors and egoism, our ignorance, insensitivity, and half-knowledge. So, in a sense, each one of us follows the track of the hero, driven onward by some unconscious quest for fulfillment, some hidden law of our being.

Whether we like it or not, we must cross many thresholds of change. As heroes, courageous or timid, we must pursue our quest for new being. What the classical hero called "adventure," we call "crisis." We do not consciously select our crises, but something inside us, some psychic element or force has to devise the specific circumstances needed to wake us. I believe we tap an unceasing spring of courage and confidence when we know that our crises may arrive at more or less predictable times as stages in our emergence. More than likely we have to encounter and assimilate some kind of suffering before we pass over the thresholds separating completion and advance.

Death and rebirth are a central motif of mythology, initiation, and biography. Psychological crises tend to occur at the beginnings and the ends of the seven-year cycles, and in many cases the halfway points are marked by some kind of change or disturbance, i.e., at ages thirty-five, thirty-eight and a half, forty-two. We will look at this later in the chapter.

Every kind of psychological crisis is a *process in time*. For example, subliminal changes occur in the psyche long before they reach the surface as a crisis. Many people notice a marked alteration in their dream life; their dreams often become more abundant and vividly intense. It later is apparent that the change in dream life was a prelude to an approaching crisis. Obviously, something is happening in levels below the waking mind. This stage is followed, more often than not, by a period of restlessness and disorientation when old certainties blur and dissolve. The whole process may be triggered by a death, accident, illness, or marital upheaval. This is when synchronicity plays a vital role.

Joseph L. Henderson and Maude Oakes, in their book, *The Wisdom of the Serpent*, describe the archetypal crisis as a threefold process of "separation, transition, and incorporation." The first phase is noted for its feeling of withdrawal and isolation, as we lose our bearings and suffer a gnawing discontent. As the inner turbulence increases, our anguish may reach panic proportions, which alienates us from friends or family. At such times, we may also be divided against ourselves. Feeling unprotected against fate, we become, for a while, "displaced" persons. No matter how hard we try, we cannot escape our predicaments by rationalizing them. Some make desperate but fruitless attempts to escape into work or pleasure, but the relentless change continues during the transition. Some stand in the eye of their storm, bereft of either anchor or compass, peering into the depths of their own abyss. The abating crisis leaves us numbed and will-less, yet strangely detached and at peace. Eventually, the passing of time pulls us over the threshold, and we can confidently expect the return of our lost enthusiasm and vigor; this is the "incorporation" or reorganization stage when the new experiences are "digested" and incorporated. We have passed through the purging fire. We are different, freer, more awake to ourselves and to our environment.

In some cases, the crisis may be severe enough to threaten the disintegration of the personality. Generally speaking, however, most of the psychological upheavals typical of the seven-year cycle run their course in a lower key. They are nevertheless symptomatic of the difficult and painful emergence of a new sense of self. It is indeed a remorseless process; some obscure force in the psyche gives us no choice—these cycles of becoming, this helix of change, must turn. The worm must turn—but it is a glowworm!

Once Upon a Time: Seven in the Fairy Tales

Laurens van der Post in his moving book *The Heart of the Hunter* states that the Bushman of Southern Africa knew intuitively that without a story his life had no frame of reference to the whole, he had no clan or family: without a story of one's own, no individual life; without a story of stories, no life-giving continuity with the beginning and therefore no future. Life for him was living a story.

To further enlarge the personality of the seven, we will examine its vital significance in the fairy tale. Our ancestors lovingly held on to the precious myths and tales which fortified and guided them along their odyssey of time. Their education was largely dependent on these pictorial maps of the path to maturity. Multidimensional in meaning, artful in construction, the old tales were created by the imagination of the sage and spread abroad by the "teachers"—the storytellers.

Myth, legend, and folktale depict the psychological route to egohood by signposting the stages and marking the dangers which await the traveler. In other words, the tale is essentially an archetypal picture of a biographical process. The fairy tale prepares children for the stages of their growing up, their movement toward independence. The fairy tale forecasts the ominous thresholds at age seven, at puberty, and at egohood, and keeps children in touch with their own incorruptible and eternal reality, which otherwise tends to be eclipsed by the child's immersion in the physical world.

But why are these old stories so durable? What is the reason for their irrepressible vitality? First, just as it is for our children, the pictorial idiom was perfectly suited to the nonintellectual, prelogical mind of the ancient. Second, the dramatic and emotional content easily engages the attention. Not only does the story stimulate the imagination, it also appeals to the child's love of action, and provides healthy emotional exercise. Above all, it implants pictures of the track to independence. We adults should remember that the gateway to a child's soul is not barred by fences of skepticism and cynicism. Pictures, unlike concepts and cold, hard, indigestible facts, appeal to the child's fantasy and are therefore easily absorbed and digested. The pictures are not obliterated but percolate through layers of memory into the interior life, where they become healing, integrating forces which strengthen the emerging personality. They give the child a *sense of path.*

Some adults shrink from giving their children the more disturbing tales. But removing the blood and guts from genuine tales to serve them with sugar and cream is a contemptible practice. Of course, we should select our stories with great care and respect for the child's temperament, but death, suffering, and adversity are basic features in our journey through time. Pruning all the grimness and horror, I suspect, puts children at a disadvantage. They will find it more difficult to accept the pain and death of real life, whereas children reared on real folk-wisdom have something in them which senses the meaning. After all, death in the tale does not refer to mortal death, but, rather to the loss of childhood and the gain of maturity.

With this in mind, we will look at some specific examples of how fairy tales illuminate the psychological character of the seven. The protective union of child, mother, and environment begins to disintegrate toward the end of the first seven-year

period, when the child experiences itself as a separate entity
among other independent entities. This differentiation of self
from the world means that the child must learn to *share* the
world with others. The idyllic dream world is doomed the
moment the story child leaves home to meet the dangers in the
forest. In real life, this picture reminds us of our first step to
independence: the challenge of school.

Some tales point to the first seven-year span, while others
deal with the thresholds of puberty (fourteen) and egohood
(twenty-one). For example, the English tale, "The Stars in the
Sky" depicts the period between seven and fourteen. Our fourteen-year-old spends all her time crying for her beloved stars,
which in this case represent the blissful unity I mentioned earlier. So she runs away from home to search for them in
nature—in brook, millpond, and meadow. Assisted by a horse
and a fish who lead her to a rainbow, she attempts to climb her
way back to the stars. Alas, the height makes her dizzy, and she
falls. Wakened by the shock, she finds herself lying on the floor
beside her bed! The dream is over; she is fourteen, and puberty
means that she is now a resident of earth, not heaven.

Many tales go further and point out the dangers of puberty,
particularly sexuality and the lure of material possessions. Adolescents are able to think independently and can grasp knowledge of the physical world. Many tales therefore warn them
beforehand not to become *too* earthbound, *too* embroiled in
their senses, lest they lose sight of their spiritual origin and
reality. They must beware of the witch who would imprison
them in the lofty towers of the brain. That dreaded old crone is
nothing less than the chilly and deadening world of the intellect, divorced from the warmth of feeling and conscience.

Fairy tales, however do not condemn the cleverness of
thought. The story of the audacious little tailor who cleverly
stitches his thoughts together shows the value of cleverness
and how easy it is to deceive clumsy, half-witted giants. Many

stories use the picture of spinning and weaving to represent thinking. The fourteen-year-old Sleeping Beauty, for example, pricks her finger on the spindle of thought and loses consciousness of her spiritual nature. She "dies" to childhood.

Adolescence brings with it a new feeling of independence, but also of temptation. Hansel and Gretel, after leaving home, discover a gingerbread and candy house in the middle of the forest. Their awakening desires, their fascination for the sweetness of life, tempts them to nibble at it. The evil witch within nearly devours them, but she is thwarted by their cleverness. Thus Hansel and Gretel, by applying their thinking, are able to return home bearing the witch's treasure.

The much-loved adventures of Snow White provide children with exceptional pictures of the seven-year steps to maturity. Snow White's natural mother, the protective, maternal aspect of motherhood, is replaced by the stepmother, who in fairy tale language, personifies the aggressive, domineering, and possessive side of femininity. So the queen, demonstrating the dark side of desire, plots to kill her stepdaughter who is as beautiful as a spring day and fairer than the queen herself. But the compassion of the huntsman foils the queen, and Snow White continues her journey to adolescence. Her discovery of the seven dwarves with their seven mountains, seven beds, seven plates and seven candles, marks another stage of her emergence. The path through the forest leads her into the world, where she has to *serve* the dwarves by cooking and cleaning; she has to *share* their world.

Once Snow White has passed the threshold of the seventh year, she has to face the cunning queen during the struggle through puberty. Despite the protection of the dwarves, she is tempted by her awakening desires. The disguised queen laces Snow White's bodice so tightly that it restricts her breathing and makes her lose consciousness. The lungs and heart form the physical foundation of feelings, so this picture tells us that Snow

White is cut off from the dreamy, feeling-dominated life of pre-adolescence. Although she is revived by the dwarves, she then has to face the temptation of the poisoned comb and apple. She discards another quality of her childhood when her head touches the poisoned comb of logical thinking, and her bite of the poisoned apple of sexuality concludes her passage through puberty. Lying in her glass coffin, wept over by owl, raven, and dove, the ancient symbols for wisdom, intuition, and love, Snow White is eventually awakened by a kiss from the prince, who represents her own emergent ego. This happy union represents the achievement of adulthood at twenty-one; it signifies the union of body, soul, and spirit. What happens to the queen? She, alas, is condemned to dance to her death in red-hot slippers made of iron. Does she not represent the negative, one-sided aspect of personality which loses itself in the superficial *mirror* of appearances, or in the wild dance of desire which kills all sense of reality? It is not difficult to intuit the meaning if we know that the incidents and characters represent psychological aspects of the human personality and its seven-year cycles of development.

For a deeper understanding of the relationship between fairy tales and the physiological, psychological, and spiritual dynamics unfolding within the seven-year phases of childhood and adolescence, the reader should examine Rudolf Steiner's educational lectures. The highly meaningful connection between folklore and childhood development is well understood by the Waldorf school movement, where it is a vital ingredient in the curriculum of the early grades.

The First Seven Years: Trailing Clouds of Glory

With the fairy tales in mind, we can attempt a clearer understanding of the path to adulthood by briefly sketching the seven-year stages of development from a physiological and a psychological point of view.

What do we mean when we say that a child "grows up"? "Growing down" is perhaps a more descriptive phrase since it better illustrates the way the self gradually penetrates body and soul and enters mortal space and time. Basically, our "I," the core of our uniqueness, takes twenty-one years to master all the primary functions of body and soul. To understand this miraculous process, we must first recognize the twin streams of *growth* and *consciousness* which lead us to physical and mental independence.

Although it takes the ego about twenty-one years to gain control of body and soul, its influence is present from the beginning. Even before birth, mothers can sense the irrepressible drive behind the embryo's intention to live and grow. This thrust dominates the first three years of the child's physical growth. Gradually, however, the baby's energies become more and more involved in psychological expansion, in the psyche's determination to act, to experience, to become conscious of itself. Mother knows full well that this relentless force will drive her child away from her toward adolescence and independence.

The baby's head at birth is almost full sized, while the rest of the body has yet to develop. It is easy to see where the forces of growth are concentrated. But these proportions soon alter when the forces of growth press downward, pushing, so to speak, the chest and limbs away from the head. The expansion of growth is simultaneous with another line of development: the sequential stages of standing, walking, speaking, and thinking, which represent the emerging consciousness. Any weakness or retardation in one stage tends to impair subsequent stages. That is why the first three years are immensely important for the life span as a whole. Readers interested in this sequence will find Dr. Karl König's book *The First Three Years of the Child* of great value. The physical instruments we use to act, feel, and think determine much of the quality of our adult life. Many adults become ill in their prime, just when they are poised to convert all their training and experience into a meaningful contribution to life. Many of the organic roots of disease are embedded in the formative years between birth and seven, the period when children transform the genetic "model" of their bodies into their own property.

Many educators and parents too easily forget that the early childhood is built from feelings, imagination, fantasy, and dreams. Seduced by the mania of progress, they believe they should push for intellectual maturity as early as possible. Oblivious of the dangers, they overextend the child's nerve system, undermining both physical and emotional development. This sort of brain worship weakens the infant's health and freezes its natural creativity. Such abuse can lead to ill health, mental problems, and even premature senility. Early childhood should be sacrosanct, left untouched by all educators except those who leave their intellects behind when they step into the refreshing play world of stories, games, fantasy, and imitation.

Childhood is a series of separations. As we grow, so we gradually lose the union of self, family, and world. This is the only way we can establish a conscious and independent relationship to life. Our early appetite for life urges us to grasp the physical world with our senses. Thus, the joyful imagination of play, touching, tasting, running, speaking, etc., develops our orientation and self-mastery. Likewise, grazed knees, quarrels over toys, and disputes over bedtimes are the collisions with life which engender both a self and a social awareness.

The threshold between six and seven is marked physically by the appearance of the permanent teeth—the densest components in the human body. On the other hand, it signifies the beginning of a new phase of consciousness. According to Rudolf Steiner, the formative activity which has hitherto been involved with building the child's physical body is now partially released from this task to stimulate the development of psychological activity.

Seven to Fourteen: from Light to Shadow

The forces of growth in this period are first located in the respiratory organs before they move down to the organs of reproduction. Accordingly, this vital cycle of childhood is responsible for the enlargement of heart and lungs, the four-to-one ratio of pulse and breath, and sexual maturity. Of course, the whole child is growing, but the *degree* of growth, of expansion, depends on the age of the child—it is not everywhere uniform. In the first half of this period, the expansion is more pronounced in the chest cavity, while the second half is concerned with the sex organs and lengthening limbs. Physical growth notwithstanding, we could also say that before seven the developmental emphasis is centered on physical activity, while between seven and fourteen it shifts to emotional and then mental levels.

This period is ruled by feelings. Children, therefore, need to exercise their feelings; they want to *feel* life during this supersentient, supersubjective time of fear, anticipation, joy, and sadness. Thus, for a while, they are submerged in a bubbling cauldron of feelings which they cannot yet judge or control. Also, in this period of emotional expansion and awakening of intellectual activity, the child's role models are of crucial importance. It is through the role model that the innate drive of the self translates experience into the manifestation of personality.

The child's development in this cycle is profoundly influenced by education—for good or ill. Bearing in mind the particular sensitivity of soul in this cycle, the educator would be well advised to introduce the child to the world by first translating the world into pictorial, feeling-imbued terms. Few educators recognize the tremendous potential in the first half of this period. On the contrary, the intrusion which many call "education" merely marches legions of sterile facts across the fertile garden of imagination and feeling. No wonder the stunted feeling life of so many adults requires multitudes of psychiatrists to solve problems which should never have arisen. An education which takes into account the need for "emotional exercise" helps to promote a healthy emotional rapport between intellect and emotions, and between self and social world. During this second seven-year cycle, children become more self-conscious, more centered, more analytical. The amazing mental expansion about the twelfth year means that youngsters can now deal with more intellectual material. Their maturing sense of space enables them to understand geometry and geography, their sense of time makes history meaningful, and their sense of cause and effect enables them to tackle the sciences.

The onset of puberty near the end of this cycle is often marked by a loss of natural grace, laughter, and openness. Young teenagers become more introverted, hidden, and isolated. Preoccupied with a startling new awareness of themselves, they can be secretive, hostile to criticism, moody, and easily embarrassed. This is the telltale time of blushing! This self-consciousness and sensitivity may well erode the communication between parent and young person. Our teenagers feel things very deeply, and it will take a while for them to become comfortable with themselves. The advent of sexuality makes them acutely aware of their own bodies, but it also signifies the "coming to ground," the death of childhood and the birth of independence. Even as the body grows stronger, denser, heavier—more and more a prisoner of gravity—the mind is opening to the limitless universe of ideas, ideals and meaning.

Primitive peoples regarded puberty as a form of dying, a threshold which some observed by burying their children in

ceremonial graves. Through such rites the candidates celebrated their rebirth and acceptance into tribal society. Indeed,
some tribes give their adolescents new names to represent this
new identity.

A young fourteen-year-old friend dreamed a particularly
vivid dream which clearly symbolized her immersion in
puberty. She remembered standing on a crowded beach—but it
was a beach made of concrete! The sun, which was white and
very brilliant, dazzled everyone else, but she could see that it
was suspended by a thread. She recalled the blissful feeling of
swimming, but when she swam around the sinking disk, she
saw its dark and ominous side. Perhaps she saw (to use a Jun-
gian phrase) the shadow side of her own emergent self. The
radiant sun of childhood sank into the symbolic waters of her
unconscious psyche. Or to change the picture slightly, the light
of childhood was eclipsed by the shadow of earthly maturity.
This is typical of the pubertal rite of passage, the entrance into
another degree of self-identity.

Fourteen to Twenty-one: the Flush of Independence

Physical development reaches its conclusion between ages
fourteen and twenty-one in the extremities of the upper and
lower limbs. But physical growth during those years is less
conspicuous than the explosion of consciousness; teenagers'
rapidly maturing mental faculties enable them to concentrate
for long hours, digesting staggering amounts of intellectual
data. Inwardly, however, our teenagers struggle to fathom their
emotions and come to terms with the exciting but disquieting
expansion of their sexuality. They are also obliged to relate
their subjective awareness of themselves to the outside world of
high school, college, job, and personal relationships. Naturally,
the adjustment to independence reduces the unconditional trust

they once had for adults; they still need advice and role models, but the source must command their respect. There can be skepticism, even cynicism, in this age of intolerance. Secretly hypercritical of themselves, teenagers can be outrageously critical of others, quick to draw premature conclusions and to adopt uncompromising stances. Like the heroes of mythology, they cut the umbilical family cords and reach out toward freedom. This sometimes becomes an overactive rebellion against all authority. Most of the momentum of this expansion will depend on the quality of the self-image and self-worth formed in the earlier cycles.

Besides the competitive demands made by education, career, and peer groups, teenagers are now more aware of the flaws in their temperament and upbringing. Also, the enhanced sense of their own uniqueness may make them feel uneasy and restless in social situations. On one hand, they recognize their individuality; on the other, they seek to balance this aloofness by congregating in groups they can identify with. This new feeling of self and the sense of isolation brings with it a need for community and the desire for relationships with the opposite sex. Toward the end of this period, when the ego has emerged from its whirlpool of feelings, it begins to yearn for personal meaning. Young persons begin to contemplate the meaning of their existence.

We have seen how each of the first three seven-year cycles produces a different quality of consciousness. We could sum them up by comparing the way a child, an adolescent, and a young adult might react to the death of a parent. Very young children experience the loss on a subliminal, organic, mostly unconscious level. They would not think about it or analyze their emotions. Little might be visible on the surface, but this would not mean that the separation would not affect their health and personality later. One might go as far as to say that it is built into their physiology. Adolescents, on the other hand, *feel* their loss very deeply. In fact, their pain tends to swamp the self, because the emotional reactions in this period are very intense and obvious. Of course, I am speaking very broadly, considering that one young person may be driven inwardly while another rebels outwardly. It is a matter of temperament. Young adolescents are deeply affected by grief, but their awakening thought-life struggles to come to terms with it. Young adults are also engulfed by their anguish, but their consciousness enables them to look more objectively at their own feelings and at the feelings of others. Indeed, their pain may prompt them to explore the mystery of life and death and its philosophical-religious implications.

As twenty-one-year-olds, they stand poised on the launch pad of independent life, bearing the mandate of their own responsibility. In the simplest terms, their individuality has fashioned itself a physical body and psyche which can think, feel, and act for itself. From now on, the process of growth and consciousness is reversed. Up to now, most of the formative energy has poured into the unfolding of the physical body. From now on, the body will follow a hardening, devitalizing route while consciousness continually adds to itself through the pursuit of self-knowledge, experience, and the search for meaning.

Many a twenty-one-year-old is given a symbolic key of independence to mark the special occasion. This gift echoes the medieval rites of initiation celebrated by all twenty-one-year-old knights. The long arduous preparations for knighthood were solidly based on a view of human development which clearly recognized the seven-year stages. For example, male children up to the age of seven were called "knaves." Suitable seven-year-old candidates selected from the noble class were placed in the care of a preceptor knight. The little "page," no matter how illustrious his ancestry, had to learn the basic lesson of humility by serving in the refectories and waiting at table. Besides his menial duties, he was taught certain codes of behavior and instructed in hunting, dancing, and music. Between fourteen and twenty-one, the adolescent "esquire" had to master the social graces of singing, dancing, and conversation. Even more important, he was encouraged to deepen his moral awareness and respect for womankind. These disciplines introduced him to the highest ideals of knighthood, while his combat training developed his physical prowess and courage. With the satisfactory completion of his physical, mental, and spiritual instruction, the twenty-one-year-old could prepare for the sacred ceremony of initiation. Dressed in white, he affirmed the ideals of his rank and accepted his spurs, gauntlets, shield, mail, and lance. The celebration reached its climax when the young knight accepted the accolade and the dedicated sword. Sworn to bring compassion and justice to all the evil places in his life's path, and armed with both material and spiritual weapons, he was permitted to leave the sanctuary and follow his quest and destiny.

Twenty-one to Twenty-eight: the Chase of Experience

Does twenty-one signify the end and conclusion of the seven-year progression? There is an overwhelming array of evidence to suggest that this rhythm continues to unfold until death. We should realize, however, that the degree of psychological advancement, especially after twenty-eight, is no longer automatic but depends largely on our own efforts. I do not believe that the development of the psyche ever stops completely, inasmuch as the seven-year cycles continue to regulate the "digestion" of experience, by which the outward experience becomes part of the inward self. But those who strive for self-knowledge and meaning obviously fulfill more of their potential in each seven-year span than those who do not—and they better transform their past experience.

We may call the effervescent cycle between twenty-one and twenty-eight "the period of enthusiasm and intemperance." It is the time when we celebrate our liberation from the somber introversion of adolescence by shaking our tail feathers at the world. Regardless of the cost, young adults spend prodigious amounts of energy searching for physical, emotional, and intellectual challenge and stimulation, accepting privation and sacrifice as a matter of course. They experiment with their newfound independence, testing and proving themselves, doing almost any crazy thing in the name of experience. In this process, the newly awakened self, swept along by the winds of optimism, tends to be flooded by a welter of impressions, all of which have to be digested later. At that pace we are easily fooled by the blandishments of pleasure and the counterfeit values of the seductive world. The voice of conscience, though stronger than it was in adolescence, is often smothered by the roar of action. On the other hand, the awakening sense of social responsibility drives many a flushed knight full tilt at the dragons of injustice and hypocrisy. These radical lances, however, are seldom tempered by perspective and wisdom. It is the exercise and experience of battle that counts as the young ego finds itself by pitting itself against the world.

For some, however, these venturesome years are far from happy, especially when the ego has been enclosed in an overprotective family sheath with little opportunity for self-expression and independence. Those who carry their adolescence into this period soon devise some form of identity crisis to wake them and expand their definitions of themselves.

This exploratory phase of life tempts us to taste the bittersweet fruit of the world. This is why ideals can become all-powerful forces at this susceptible time in our lives, although it is their emotional impact and appeal which makes them so irresistible. Consequently, it is natural to investigate weird and tantalizing philosophies and lifestyles, even though we rarely adopt them.

Likewise, our need for the emotional and intellectual food offered by human relationships plays a major role in this period. Some of us are profoundly influenced by older people who have achieved a firm standpoint in life; others discover a special sense of belonging with their peers. No less important is the emotional experience arising from serious romantic relationships. In love as in ideals, there are ecstasies and heartbreaks, false paths and dead ends, but the exercise of liberty prepares the still-emerging self for a greater challenge—destiny!

Many sense some sort of inner change, especially toward the end of this period when the cycle swings from its active to its passive pole. We seem to run out of steam; the pace of life slackens, and some of our former pleasures, loves, and ideals lose their allure. Euphoria turns into disenchantment. We may become more introspective and feel differently about ourselves. We are not so sure we know who we are after all, although we sense our individuality more than we did at twenty-one. We look more intently at our achievements and failures, evaluating our personal relationships, our careers and personalities. This mood points to subtle changes in the psyche which forewarn us of the approaching threshold at twenty-eight. Obviously, there is a time for tasting life and a time for digesting it. All the experience gathered in this cycle must be assimilated and integrated for the emerging personality to evolve further.

At the close of this cycle we may feel stuck and need some kind of crisis to break the status quo. Henri Troyat, noting this period in the life of Dostoevsky, remarks that Dostoevsky was *waiting* for the crisis which threw him into prison six months before his twenty-eighth birthday. As Troyat, in his book *Firebrand: The Life of Dostoevsky*, points out, Dostoevsky did not bewail his misfortune; rather he felt relief. For some time he had felt the urgent need for a disaster of some kind, a tragedy to blast him out of his useless and indolent life. His imprisonment,

therefore, served to shatter the frozen monotony of his existence. Now he could breathe again, now he could wake up to
himself. This sharp slap of destiny brought him to his senses
and to a new beginning—it was a crucial threshold.

In the life of Charles Darwin, this period also was particularly significant. He was twenty-one when he embarked on his
famous voyage in the *Beagle* which took him among the
Southern Islands and along the coasts of South America and
Australasia. From December 1831 to October 1836, the young
naturalist observed, recorded, and collected enough new material for a lifetime of research. His mind and notebooks stuffed
with exciting data, he returned home to digest the information.
At twenty-eight, he began his research into the origin of species, but his vague, unformed ideas would take years of care-
ful synthesis and testing before he could present his theory. As
with Darwin, so it is with all of us. The experience we gather
in one cycle has to be properly assimilated and worked on by
the psyche before it can change our consciousness later in life.

To better evaluate the changes possible around the twenty-
eight-year threshold, the reader would do well to study the
period between twenty-one and twenty-eight in the life of William James, who later made significant contributions to American psychology. This period was so miserably burdened by
psychological discomfort and a host of physical ailments that
he seriously considered suicide. Despite his travels abroad to
take the various "cures," he returned to his homeland as
despondent as ever. He reached his lowest ebb as his twenty-
eight-year threshold approached. But the tide turned when he
discovered the re-creative, generative power of his own will. In
one of his notebooks of his twenty-eighth year, he announced
that he had faced and overcome his crisis. His first act of will
was to believe in his own self-will. He decided to abstain from
speculations and put his efforts into cultivating these feelings of
moral freedom. Hitherto, suicide seemed to be the only way he

could act courageously, but now he believed in his own individual reality and creative power. He had reached his turning point. This surge of will, this leap in self-awareness, released the psychological pressures blocking his relationship to himself. The health of his body and mind improved rapidly, followed by the expansion of intellectual power and the flowering of his personality. The end of his crisis is marked by his entrance into the academic world soon after his thirtieth year. This example illustrates the fact that our psychic thresholds can indeed affect mental health. It suggests also that many of our physical ailments have a psychosomatic connection to the seven-year cycles.

Twenty-eight to Thirty-five: Adjusting the Course

For most people, the crucial years between twenty-eight and thirty are particularly trying and can be a time of disorientation, stress, or even dramatic change. We enter a phase of *contraction*, and our inward-looking self-assessment primes us for the vital expansion which takes place close to the thirtieth year. Opportunities seemed to appear out of thin air in the previous cycle, but now life demands more exacting and thought-filled decisions in keeping with our emergent sense of self and our social responsibilities. The realization that we are now much more dependent on our own inner resources may make us anxious and unconfident for a time. Although we get less help from the external world, some kind of inborn stimulus in the psyche exhorts us to face ourselves on a deeper level. We are forced to reconsider our position: how and where do we fit into life? Are we on the right course? There are, of course, an infinite number of variations to this theme, but broadly speaking, the internal pressures making us restless and uncomfortable around twenty-eight precipitate a crisis sometime between twenty-eight and thirty. This inner turbulence may be synchronized with an illness, conflict, or separation of some kind. This immensely significant turning point in life will be discussed at length in the following chapter.

At thirty, we have a past that we can look back upon and evaluate. Besides the disconcerting feeling of estrangement which represents our break with the past, many people are blessed with new and fruitful personal relationships at this time. Once the problems of the thirtieth year are overcome and the pace of life accelerates again, we settle down to the tasks at hand. Cautiously optimistic about our future and confident in our ability to make good, we adjust to new patterns of living. Many of us take on more responsibility and financial obligations as we climb the ladder of our ambition in this generative, competitive, and generally acquisitive phase of life. But this outer growth and the hardening routines of home and work tend to mask continuing changes in the psyche. The momentum of these productive years may obscure our deeper longings and our weaknesses because we have little time to develop a real rapport with ourselves or with others—life is just too busy, too outward. The seeds of future crises are being planted at this time.

Take marriage, for example. More than likely, matrimonial bliss will fade somewhat as husband and wife grow used to each other and settle into their respective roles. By now, they have probably worked out a practical routine of family life. Marriage being a multilevel relationship with physical, emotional, and spiritual overtones, tensions can be expected to arise from the emerging egos of husband and wife. This is all the more probable if the man has repressed his deeper feelings or built barricades of insensitivity to protect his inner life from the burdensome rat race.

Most women undergo some form of self-emergence between twenty-eight and thirty-five when the ego begins to work more intensely within the personality. A woman may no longer allow herself to be molded by circumstance or tradition to fit a role which denies her emerging individuality. She becomes aware of another level of independence which recognizes her right to personal fulfillment. Obviously, this insistent "new" self has to adjust to the family milieu. But can the husband learn to communicate with his "new" wife? Can she, in turn, help to melt the frozen crust of his perhaps desensitized feeling life? Failure to recognize and express their changing attitudes will eventually inhibit the ripening of their relationship. Marriage obeys that law of life which states that a relationship which cannot transform itself destroys itself. Thus, the living process of marriage breaks down if it cannot, in time, become a true partnership of egos. A stagnant marriage literally produces "stale mates," and the egos diverge instead of achieving new levels of union. It may be possible to smooth over or ignore the crises brewing during this period, but they will return with a vengeance in the next cycle. Of course, much depends on the age difference, especially if the partners are in different seven-year periods.

What then is happening in the psyche between twenty-eight and thirty-five? Infants are unaware of their own egos, but adults are self-conscious; not only do we recognize our own ego, we have learned to relate it to the egos of others. This statement, however, is true only insofar as individuals are acquainted with their own authentic self. Remember that our trail to independence took us through three basic levels of consciousness of childhood and the waking consciousness of adolescence. But the term "waking consciousness" covers a wide range of awareness stretching from the mindfulness needed to drive a car to the superconsciousness of the mystic. Now our level of wakefulness determines how deeply and clearly we perceive our own ego. Our level of wakefulness, however, is never fixed; not only does it fluctuate during the day, it changes as we grow older.

This chapter suggests that the seven-year cycle is essentially an "ego rhythm" seated in the nocturnal depths of the self which continues to work on one's personality throughout life. In other words, one's attitude to oneself and to life should be qualitatively different in each of the seven-year periods. This subtle development in our awareness is reflected in the quality of our thinking. As our self-consciousness deepens, thinking establishes greater autonomy over our feelings and actions. Between twenty-eight and thirty-five, thought begins to occupy the judgement seat where it can overview the experiences which stormed the psyche in the previous period. Its light begins to cut away some of the illusions which festoon the personality, since we have by now plenty of experience which can be examined and assessed in terms of our ideals, goals, and conscience. So, all things considered, we should have a more thoughtful and realistic picture of ourselves by the time we reach thirty-five.

Thirty-five to Forty-two: under Self-power

This cycle, for the most part, continues the major expansion begun at thirty. The conversion of our psychic potential into reality depends on our own efforts. Our development, the deepening of our humanity, is now a matter of fate or freedom—it is our choice.

Many readers would claim that they notice nothing particularly unusual happening to them at thirty-five—or any of the other seven-year points, for that matter—but this does not preclude the possibility of internal adjustments occurring at such times. After all, how many of us are aware of subtle changes taking place in our consciousness? How closely do we monitor our inner life, especially when our condition appears normal and we are fully preoccupied with the business of living? Generally speaking, we are not exposed to the subliminal world of the psyche and its rhythmic tides, except for the occasional surge which influences our dreams, feelings, and intuitions, or when the untransformed past erupts in our present and demands attention.

The consciousness which tells me I am an individual represents only the first step to my psychological independence—or so the poets, sages, and seers have told us from time immemorial. Obviously, their insight reveals a more detailed picture of their personal reality than of ours, which is foggy and incomplete. Yet despite our inner blindness, we have enough consciousness and common sense to recognize bits and pieces of our own reality, and we know that this is somehow connected to our search for meaning. Carl Gustav Jung said, "Human consciousness created objective experience and meaning, and man found his indispensable place in the great process of being." But surely everyone has to make this discovery through a slow and sometimes painful process of living.

During this cycle, we are still more interested in the future than in the past and we are not yet unduly disturbed by the growing gap between our expectations and our actual performance and achievements. Although our goals may be unrealistic, we give no thought to renouncing our potential. In the preceding period, the turning point at thirty was largely conditioned by the psychological change at twenty-eight. Likewise, in many lives the mental change at thirty-five may not manifest itself as an outer change until thirty-six or later. We will consider this in detail when we come to the twelve-year cycle.

Despite the expansive character of this cycle, we can expect some form of tension, particularly at the beginning, the middle, and the end. The more we become "habit-trapped," the more automatonlike our responses, the less we are aware of the demands of our still-emerging self. The psyche, more than likely, will devise some form of crisis to break us free from our straitjackets. We may hasten to blame life for our misfortunes, but our crises obey the law of our being—we have them when we need them. Worldly success and its self-inflation mean little on this level. A rapid climb to wealth or prestige will have added plenty of new illusions to those we already have, and a setback may be needed to clear a space for reassessment. Crises may take the form of marital conflict, illness, "accident," or blighted hopes, but the real causes, more often than not, are internal. The stress may be acute enough to force a change of course or even what is euphemistically labeled a "nervous breakdown." These internal pressures are likely to reach crisis proportions halfway through this period, at about thirty-eight and a half. Indeed, many people have a rough time of it between thirty-eight and forty-two.

The pattern of these rhythms suggests that thirty-five, thirty-eight, and forty-two are critical points where interior change presses upward into our waking life. This intervention from below can cause severe disruption. Take, for the example, the extreme case of Vincent van Gogh, who failed to fully complete the psychic transition from adolescence to adulthood and was driven to suicide at age thirty-seven. Van Gogh's terrible psychic disturbance at thirty-five was more than his constitution could handle. His disabled ego, undermined by years of acute depression, malnutrition, exposure, and alcohol, was incapable of transforming his chaotic yet sensitive and vigorous personality. His earnestness, moral sense, and desperate desire to serve and be loved were swamped by a ferocious temper and fits of despair and self-loathing. Bitterly divided against himself, van Gogh could not control his intense and disruptive emotions nor come to terms with his awakening spiritual perceptions. He might have managed it had his health not been so eroded by years of physical neglect and hardship.

Van Gogh, from all accounts, must have been a rather startling character with his glittering eyes and bristling red hair.

Thoroughly confused and lost between twenty-one and twenty-eight, he searched furiously for love and meaning, but met only disappointment and rejection. His amorous hopes failed to materialize, and even the wretchedly ill prostitute he nursed for a time eventually turned him out. He tried to enter the priesthood, but what could the Church do with such a temperament? Society had no place for him. Yet his letters show that he knew he had something of worth in him. He saw himself as a bird in a cage, but he knew he was changing—he saw himself in a molting period. Van Gogh realized that this harrowing period of psychological hibernation was part of his personal transformation—discovering his real identity. He felt that this painful self-discovery would lead him to a new beginning if only he could last it out.

Van Gogh began to devote all his time to art when he was twenty-eight. His childlike sensitivity could intuit something of the generative energy pulsating in nature and in the simple folk of town and country, forces akin to those raging unchecked in his own soul. Despite his emerging genius, however, peace, love, and recognition eluded him. His ego simply could not withstand his destructive habits, accentuated by his poverty and the anxiety and passion which tyrannized his inner life. He put every scrap of his being into his work. Only in that way could he force his almost perpetual depression to serve his creativity instead of utterly swamping his spirit.

Van Gogh's tempestuous worship of Paul Gauguin brought everything to a head when he was thirty-five; he cut off his own ear. His failure to build a lasting friendship based on cooperation and free from jealousy and strife drove him to this terrible act of desperation. Despite his battle to salvage the remains of his sanity at the hospital in Saint Rémy, his poor ego was shattered by its anguish, and his broken body and mental torment made self-transformation impossible and suicide inevitable.

Gauguin was thirty-five when he abandoned his job to commit himself totally to his art. He was forty-two when his distraught friend Vincent triggered his own upheaval. In fact, van Gogh's suicide and the death three months later of Theo van Gogh completely upended Gauguin's career. Heartbroken by Vincent's suicide, Theo, who was Gauguin's friend and patron, rapidly crumbled into paralysis and insanity. Thus, Gauguin's crisis at forty-two marked a major turning point in his life, for it was then that he decided to leave for Tahiti.

Albert Schweitzer had a strange connection to van Gogh although, unlike the Dutchman, Schweitzer's life was unceasingly supported by a strong sense of destination which, together with his abundant inner resources and physical vitality, carried him through this turbulent cycle. His career, up until he was thirty, was a brilliant amalgam of religion, music, and philosophy, but he then altered course to prepare for a life of medical service. After passing his final medical examinations at thirty-five, Schweitzer struggled to raise money for his African venture. He embarked for "the Dark Continent" when he was thirty-eight and a half to establish a hospital in the primeval forests of the Congo. But despite all his sacrifice and industry, at forty-two he found himself incarcerated in a European prison— in the same mental asylum once occupied by van Gogh!

In many lives, the middle of this cycle (thirty-eight and a half) appears to be crucial to the development of the cycle as a whole and is likely to be marked by important happenings. A few notable examples illustrate the difficulties which often underscore this time in life. For Marie Curie, the beginning, middle, and end were marked by synchronistic events—deaths. Her father died when she was thirty-five, her husband and scientific collaborator was killed when she was thirty-eight and a half, and her father-in-law died when she was forty-two. Franklin Delano Roosevelt suffered his crippling polio attack when he was thirty-eight, and Albert Einstein at the same age had a nervous collapse. Michelangelo was thirty-eight when his patron, Pope Julius, died; Robert Kennedy also was thirty-eight when his brother President Kennedy was assassinated. Marconi was involved in a scandal at that age and also lost the sight of one eye.

The deep-seated adjustments in the psyche during this cycle suggest that the ego is now becoming more aware of its own presence at the center of its psychological life. When Rudolf Steiner called this seven-year cycle the "period of the consciousness soul," he meant that the ego, our spiritual nucleus, can then begin to penetrate and purify our thinking, feeling, and willing. Most people are unaware of these subtle psychogenic changes, but they open the way to greater self-understanding and self-mastery. They enable us to become aware of the antagonism between the instincts and desires of our lower life and our ideal or higher self. Thus we begin to perceive ourselves in an entirely new and more objective way.

To sum up, in this cycle we can observe a subtle change in the quality of our mental relationship to ourself and to the world. The patterned methods of thinking and reaction conditioning our intellectual connection to our inner life and the outer world are less satisfactory. The self-observer senses that he is deeper and more enigmatic than he previously thought. This deepening perception stirs new doubts and hopes in the soul.

Forty-two to Forty-nine: the Dark Wood

"Midway this way of life we're bound upon, I woke to find myself in a dark wood, Where the right road was wholly lost and gone."—Dante

In many cases, forty-two brings the challenge of a fresh opportunity, a new expansion, but it also represents the psychological entrance to Dante's "dark wood of the soul "—the passage into middle age. Progress through this seven-year cycle, perhaps the most confusing and troublesome in adult life, depends largely on our previous experiences. The following observations present a rather distressing scenario of snags and thorns, but they are only possibilities. Many will negotiate their obstacles without too much trouble.

This period is crammed with all sorts of psychological phenomena, and only a far-gone materialist would try to ascribe these psychogenic changes to hormones. Even the so-called "menopausal" activity beginning in the second half of this cycle should also be considered an organic reflection of psychic change. It makes more sense to see the "change of life" as yet another example of the skin-shedding process which exposes us to another level of ourselves. Middle age is a drama of self-discovery which, more often than not, involves some kind of disorientation and a sense of emergency, sometimes a general loss of confidence and creative intellectual power.

For some, the Dark Wood is a dismal region of lost sunshine where few birds sing, but it symbolizes a vital stage of transition, an interval separating our past from our future, our youth from our old age. It is a condition darkly described by T.S. Eliot in "The Dry Savages" (written when he was forty-seven):

"Trying to unweave, unwind, unravel
and piece together the past and the future,
Between midnight and dawn, when the past is all deception,
The future futureless, before the morning watch
When time stops and time is never ending."

Life, which hitherto was inclined to thrust us into all sorts of experiences, now threatens to leave us stranded, bereft of our sense of direction. Middle age forces us to look *inward* into the mirror of ourselves—and few of us like what we see. Some are benumbed by it and others become panic-stricken; even the most buoyant of souls feel uncomfortable. Despite all past achievements, we now meet ourselves on a more fundamental level. This is where we face all those unfulfilled aspirations; this is where we ask, "Where am I? What have I done with my life?"

Many in this bleak wood shiver in the chilly winds of disenchantment. Ideas and opinions which once lifted and consoled may suddenly become stale and lifeless. Old convictions may crumble into dust just when they are needed most. This is the time of life when we uncomfortably note that much of our potential has not been fulfilled. Have we outgrown our ideals? Have we, in the struggle with our daily responsibilities, blighted our potential by discarding our once all-important ideals?

Those of us who have earned no spiritual income for years have nothing put aside for these rainy days. Our comfortable lifestyles, like our convictions, may have hardened into concrete straitjackets. In other words, we discover that we are exiles; the life we lead seems to move on another level to the one where we really exist. All things considered, life in the Dark Wood may appear to be short on options and long on uncertainty, full of agony but empty of ecstasy. Some souls have such a bad time of it that they number themselves among the living dead!

Let us then scan some of the typical aspects of the middle-age syndrome. First, though the Dark Wood may tempt us to grasp silly recipes for renewal, we should realize that middle age represents not only a psychological death but also a magnificent rebirth. We should accept the fact that our painful self-interrogation at this time is a necessary phase of self-realization. We get nowhere by grasping for our lost youth and its feckless delusions. For some of us, life has turned into a tyranny of regimentation. Many of our cherished dreams have not come true and our careers have ceased to flourish and advance. We are weary of those trendy eager beavers treading on our heels, eyes fixed on rapid promotion. ("No one seems to value experience these days!") Fresh schemes and innovations no longer spring to mind when needed. Colleagues make it to the top while we tread the same old mill of mediocrity day after day. We feel abandoned to the rubbish heap, or at best, stuck on the shelf. We know we need a lift, but change for the sake of change would be foolish.

Above all, this is a time to accept our limitations and clear out those old asphyxiating illusions and guilt we have cradled for so long. This is the time to take a frank and honest look at who and what we are. What can we still give to life? What do we really need for fulfillment? What adjustments should we make?

Shall we find consolation in our family life? Many have to accept the fact that the living process, the creative relatedness of their marriages, have been dormant for some time. Years of respectability and conformity have blocked their sensitivity and stifled all real communication. Children may have grown up, and husband and wife are thrown back upon themselves to discover just how far apart they have drifted and how little they really share. Such a home is no sanctuary for middle age but rather a comatose or vindictive mortuary of dead hopes. This psychological separation of husband and wife gives marriage a dismal and threadbare look compared to the freshness of a marriage where communication has been nurtured, a still developing partnership woven by two independent yet mutually integrated personalities.

The intense deprivation felt by some in the Dark Wood may suddenly throw their family life into disarray. Some attempt to drown their insecurity and inner barrenness with alcohol, while others abdicate their responsibility by striking out in search of their lost youth. For example, often without warning, a husband may begin wearing outlandish clothes and a trendy hairstyle. Blind to the absurdity of his behavior, this mutton-dressed-as-peacock may chase the bright young things at the office and experiment with infidelity. Such sexual protests may well wreck his marriage, no matter what its previous achievements. This alarming lunge for *La Dolce Vita*, this throwback to juvenile shallowness, represents a refusal to face the mirror, a refusal to accept the still-awakening self. Instead of maturity, we see the immoderate and self-defeating resurrection of the old complexes and traits of puberty.

Women have to contend with and adjust to their menopausal changes, while some men have to overcome the physical side of their own psychogenic changes. Both sexes, therefore, may suffer from periods of irritability, impotence, insomnia, hypochondria, and various degrees of depression. Despite these hardships, middle age is essentially a time of psychological death and rebirth. Many people view the change of life as an unwelcome invitation to senility and not maturity. Their fear of oblivion, their loss of creative hope, tempts them to see the future as nothing more than a dreadful drift to the grave. This negativism has to be countered by their own psychic resources. Those who fail to recover their sense of purpose are doomed to wander in the wood with only their phobias for company. They should see the wood for what it really is: a tremendous psychological opportunity. It is here that we tackle our shadow, the shadow which hides the beacon light of our true self. It is here we can begin to redeem the dark angel of our past. As T.S. Eliot points out in his *Hollow Men*: "Between the potency / And the existence.../ Falls the shadow."

Middle age challenges us to disperse the shadow of our psychological past, which includes all the character weaknesses and imperfections imprinted in our youth and reinforced throughout the years. It is a time for change, for self-examination and self-acceptance, a time for truth, a time to stop fooling ourselves. We should feel different when we have passed beyond the wood. Torn and tattered perhaps, but reborn out of the phoenix fire, many people feel completely reorganized and rejuvenated. Their newly found self-reliance can reshape their lifestyles and relationships because they have come to realize that real security resides not in things or other people but in the self and its sense of purpose.

Take, for example, the Russian novelist Leo Tolstoy and his psychological conflict between forty-two and forty-nine. Tolstoy's waking vision of his own death is a marvelous example of the change at forty-two, which, in this case, initiated seven years of torment that undermined his health and almost drove him to suicide. During that time, Tolstoy's sense of the meaning of life vanished altogether despite his growing family and great literary successes. He found nothing he could hold on to, nothing that could offer him peace, nothing that could silence the infernal demon of his conscience. In desperation, Tolstoy searched for any kind of religious experience which might confirm his existence and give his life relevance and meaning. Describing the change at forty-two, he recorded that something very strange was happening. He felt perplexed, lost, and dejected; his life had come to a standstill and these moments of confusion recurred at an increasing tempo. Everything he had stood for lay in shambles; he saw nothing ahead but destruction and extinction. Despite his position and talents he could no longer live; he felt compelled to rid himself of his life. Tolstoy had reached that terrifying barrier which looms between reality and Reality. It is the hinterland between the sense world and the spiritual world, between the waking mind and deeper levels of individuality. But Tolstoy also tells us that he managed to break through his threshold at the end of this cycle. Upheld by a new feeling of certainty and renewed in spirit, Tolstoy's life and writing display a distinct change of emphasis and direction. This suggests that he was inspired by the mental and moral energy released by his psychic upheaval.

Another example of this is found in the life of Rembrandt. The human soul instinctively strives to convert its experiences into new capacity, into new awareness, and Rembrandt was no exception. Rembrandt's Dark Wood was a disastrous slide into bankruptcy, which led to the auction of his prized collection, his personal belongings and even his home. But several biographers have drawn attention to the curious connection between these misfortunes and the development of his art. Despite all the anxiety and financial juggling in this period, Rembrandt's deepening religious awareness lifted his art to new heights. It was as if his creditors liberated his spirit as they stripped him of his material possessions. His uncertainty and turmoil appear to have wrought the inner changes which gave his art more insight into human nature. For example, Robert Wallace, discussing Rembrandt's portraits of that period, alludes to the fact that the artist sought models in whom he could perceive the workings of the human soul rather than the exterior characteristics of beauty or ugliness. Rembrandt, more than any other artist, worked to express the facial impress of suffering, love, redemption, and the relationship between God and humankind.

Forty-nine to Fifty-six: a Second Wind

In many lives, each seven-year point also marks the end of a particular task, a phase of activity, or a commitment of some kind. The feeling of letdown, of anticlimax, typical at these junctures, signals the psyche's need for an interval in which to digest its past and marshal its forces for a new burst of activity. A good example is Tolstoy's death vision and confusion at forty-two, following the completion of his epic labor on *War and Peace*. That period of *arrest* enabled him to absorb the previous cycle and release fresh energy and consciousness for the following stage, between forty-nine and fifty-six. A similar psychological pause can be seen in the life of Isaac Newton. After completing his great work *Principia*, written when he was forty-four and forty-five, Newton suffered a nervous disturbance which reached its climax at fifty-one. There are many striking parallels between the life and work of Newton and those of Albert Einstein. Although separated by two centuries, both were fascinated by the mysteries of light and gravity; both were inspired by unshakable belief in a universe fashioned and maintained by cosmic laws; both experienced phenomenal explosions of mental insight between twenty-three and twenty-five years of age, and both suffered breakdowns at forty-nine. Einstein's heart condition, like Newton's nervous disturbance, inserted a necessary pause for personal reassessment. Of his long convalescence in 1928, Einstein wrote: "Illness has its advantages; one begins to think, I have only just begun to think."

Michael Faraday, the brilliant English chemist and physicist, was another famous scientist troubled in body or soul at forty-nine. But all three felt refreshed in spirit and intellectual vitality when their crises abated. For example, Frank E. Manuel mentions that "Newton's crisis was followed by a dramatic reorganization of his personality and a re-channeling of his capacities that enabled him to manage his existence successfully for more than three decades."[1] Although these great men at the time may have regarded their crises as unwelcome interruptions to their work, we can evaluate their breakdowns in the light of their overall psychological development.

Obviously, the ups and downs of great individuals have a considerable bearing on humankind as a whole, while the crises we encounter from time to time affect only those close to us. Nevertheless, our personal upheavals are part of the psychological journey of the self and are just as necessary as the "crises" of birth and death.

---

1. Frank E. Manuel, *A Portrait of Isaac Newton* (Cambridge: Harvard University Press, 1968).

Our endurance and courage in this cycle depends on our inner stability and inner resources, not on the heroism of youth. Our inner gains at this time depend on our acknowledgment of what we have learned about ourselves and our acceptance of our past. Only by developing the capacity for change will we find fulfillment in the autumn and winter of our lives. On the other hand, the forlorn souls who have failed to find their way out of the Dark Wood will need all the help they can get. One notices, for example, that many cannot handle change creatively because their battered egos are too weak to provide a firm anchorage to ride out the storms. They are caught in a vicious circle; unconsciously they engineer their crises to bring them face to face with the need for change, but they are too depleted to accept the challenge. Our crises and suffering are the catalysts for the transformation which alters our relationship to ourselves and to life. No matter what our life condition, there is a compelling force in every soul which urges it to grow. An unexpected upheaval may appear to interfere with the established pattern of our lives, but on a psychic level, there is no discontinuity whatsoever.

All the old vultures of our past come home to roost somewhere in the branches of our physical and mental constitution. Body and soul now reflect all the errors and excesses of our past and we must watch out for the more extreme forms of sickness, which often strike at fifty-six or thereabouts. This, perhaps, is especially true for those who have failed to replace the vanished enthusiasm of youth with new qualities of soul and spirit. At that stage of life, many an old ideal or cherished principle, once so fresh and invigorating, is in danger of becoming hardened, dogmatic, and intolerant.

Whatever our predicaments, there is no cause for pessimism. Despite all our inner and outer wear and tear, we are still *emerging*, if only we can recognize the fact. Age offers its own unique compensations, so why envy the young? Why dwell on

wrinkles, fading appetites, and hoary failures? Do we not have
our victories? Let us stop picking the scabs of our conscience
and give ourselves a medal! Why? Despite our mental limitations and our physical frailty; despite all the catastrophes which
politicians, generals, and bureaucrats have committed in our
name; despite the cruelty of this at-times demoralizing planet;
despite the seemingly tyrannical laws of a seemingly disinterested universe; despite even those spiritual creators who con-
cocted this whirlpool of change, we have survived! We still
move forward in our time and we can call our souls our own.
Yes, we should give ourselves the tribute we deserve—give
ourselves a medal!

Fifty-six to Sixty-three: Reaping the Harvest

The crisis point at fifty-six sharply scored the life of the poet-
playwright-scientist, Johann Wolfgang von Goethe, who
reached that age in August, 1805. At the beginning of that
year he had a premonition that either he or his dear friend
Schiller would die before the year was out. Both men were ill
at the time. Their relationship is one of literature's most celebrated friendships, and each had worked in his own way to
inspire their nation through the revelation of literature and
drama. Strikingly dissimilar in physique and temperament,
they were, nevertheless, united by their ideals. Indeed, Schiller's provocative genius had inspired much of his friend's
work during the cycles between forty-two and fifty-six.
Schiller had stood at his thirty-year turning point when he met
the illustrious Goethe, and their creative liaison spanned fifteen fruitful years. The premonition proved true, and Schiller
died in May, 1805. Goethe's sense of loss cast him into the
abyss. "Half of my existence is gone from me," he wrote. "My
diary is blank at this period, the white pages intimate the

blank in my existence. In those days I took no interest in anything."This calamity, however, also coincided with the publication of the first part of *Faust*, which was undoubtedly an
autobiographical mirror of the movement of his consciousness
between twenty-one and fifty-six. His continuing work on
Faust from then on, though lacking its former fire, diffuses a
gentler glow, a deeper spirituality, reflecting the further ascent
of his consciousness. He completed the second part of *Faust*,
the fullest "confession" of his life, at the very close of his life,
at age eighty-two.

Another interesting case is that of Charles de Gaulle, whose
forty-ninth year was synchronized with the national emergency
of his nation in 1939-40, which drove him to London to direct
the French Resistance. This crucial turning point in his career
signaled his transition from soldier to politician. The rapid
ascent of his star crested in the second half of the forty-nine to
fifty-six cycle when he reentered Paris to establish himself as the
central figure in France's return to independence. But, as his
fifty-sixth year approached, de Gaulle's political fortune waned
dramatically. His reverses pushed him into a retirement which
provided a valuable period of reflection. This was when he wrote
his memoirs. So, the cycle between fifty-six and sixty-three provided a needed interlude in de Gaulle's intense career, during
which his personal destiny disengaged itself from the national
destiny of France. On a deeper level, it represented a necessary
psychological pause for inner change. De Gaulle was sixty-three
in 1953, beginning a seven-year cycle which saw the Algerian
revolt and the collapse of the Fourth Republic. During the second half of his sixty-three to seventy cycle, he was recalled to
power and given a mandate to form a new constitution. Once
again, in de Gaulle's case, the metronome of the seven was synchronized with the volatile pulse of French politics.

Most of us by age fifty-six have trimmed the sails of our
unfulfilled ambitions and unrealized hopes. During this phase

the quality of resignation indicates the level of our maturity. This spiritual resignation can sharpen one's sense of self-recognition, or it can sour the soul and blunt its appetite for the bounty of life still to come. When considering the psychological importance of this cycle, we should not forget the very special conjunction of the thirty-year and twelve-year cycles which occurs at age sixty. This cardinal point in human life represents the completion of what I have termed "the constructive period"—between thirty and sixty (see Chapter 3). It represents the portal to a more contemplative phase of life which prepares us for our final crisis—the ultimate transformation at death. Sixty, then, opens a phase of introspection where we have the opportunity to evaluate the past, plan our retirement, and acknowledge the growing specter of our own death.

The ancient Greeks regarded sixty-three as a particularly dangerous time for health. By that stage, one's physical, emotional, even moral, past is well and truly stamped on one's organic systems, and there is little we can do about it. Likewise, to some extent, our awareness, our mental clarity, and self-understanding are indications of our inner activity in the previous cycles. This implies that minds neglected for decades, untouched by curiosity, interest, or involvement, are now likely to show clear signs of degeneration and petrification. Obviously, a sterile, unquesting mind cannot release the imprisoned faculties of the psyche. Despite this apparent psychological standstill, however, development has not ceased. Even the most unawakened soul moves ever onward, shaped by events and pushed forward by the river of passing time. Sickness, bereavement, and loneliness are typical challenges which demand a response from the soul at this time of life. It is a terrible thought, but perhaps for some, suffering is the only creative element which gives meaning to their lives at this time. The last great victory is their *endurance*. Just to have entered time means that we change, be we pygmy, murderer, handicapped child, or saint.

As conscious still-evolving beings, we enjoy a valuable advantage during the autumnal stretch of our time: a sense of *process*. We are not so easily fooled into believing that every problem has a fixed and instant answer, if only we can discover it. We distrust the "experts" who mainly spend their time and our money spinning abstract solutions to problems they do not understand. Our experience helps us to realize that within every problem something is working itself out, not only on a personal level, but even on the global level. We suspect moreover, that it is the *process*, not the solution, which is important.

Older people's withdrawal from many of the temptations and superfluities of the external world further personalizes their existence—they should feel more connected to themselves. Aging helps us to sense that our biography is an inner journey through the outer world. The ultimate fact is that souls appear on earth, follow their pilgrimages, and then move on. So, we sense the real movements of life more clearly when we come to old age, the sanctuary where our center of gravity shifts from body to soul and our attachment to the mortal world lessens. If aging represents a process of physical decrease and spiritual increase, then sixty-three is a door to new opportunities no less important than the one we opened at twenty-one.

The conscious mind is a matchless analytical instrument. The psyche, on the other hand, in its invisible depths, can be thought of as a master of synthesis, and the development of the self is totally dependent on the psyche's complicated process of assimilation. All our experience, the reactions and conflicts which come to us by way of the external world, sinks into this interior cauldron of synthesis. It is there that experience is distilled and assimilated into the self. Cycle after cycle, our thoughts, feelings, and actions are the seeds planted in the inner continuum of the psyche, and in our sixties we begin to reap the harvest.

To illustrate the natural ripening of the psyche and its life's task between sixty and sixty-three, let us take a glance at the life of Alfred Nobel (1833-1896). Nobel was the famous industrial magnate who revolutionized the explosives industry by taming nitroglycerine. He was thirty when he and his family were shattered by the death of his brother Emil, who was killed while experimenting with the volatile explosive. His father suffered a stroke soon afterward, and Alfred took the helm of the family business. After his invention of dynamite and later the detonator cap, the production of dynamite climbed rapidly during the restless and nerve-wracking cycle between his thirty-fifth and forty-second years. Always in motion, Nobel traveled the length and breadth of the globe, protecting his patents, building new factories, and replacing others wrecked by accidents. His ever improving explosives placed unprecedented power in the hands of men and made possible such engineering feats as the Corinth and Panama canals. To his horror, however, Nobel saw this power also diverted to munitions, feeding the reckless ambitions of rampant nationalism. Although he worked hard to find the ultimate explosive, his hopes for a deterrent to war faded behind the acrid gunsmoke of international conflict. Thus, in a sense, his financial success and global influence became more and more at odds with his deepest aspirations. The desperate need to resolve this contradiction began to dominate his psyche in the last third of his life.

Nobel's brief but auspicious relationship with Bertha von Suttner, at the beginning of the forty-two to forty-nine cycle, was a landmark in the inner course of his life. She was his secretary for a while, and he even had hopes of a romance. But it was not to be. Although this first contact occurred long before either of them had a conscious interest in the international peace movements, Bertha, over the years, encouraged his involvement in the cause. They met again in his sixtieth year. By that time he was deeply preoccupied with the peace problem, and Bertha bombarded him with advice, literature, and appeals.

Another significant incident, a curious twist of synchronicity, marked Nobel's fifty-sixth year. His brother died but the press wrote Alfred's obituary! This bizarre error triggered intense self-examination and a pitiless review of his past achievements. The impact of this peculiar event becomes understandable if we realize that it was synchronized with the changes taking place in his psyche at that time.

Despite his incredible financial success, Nobel remained a lonely, reclusive soul, prone to soul-searching and ill health. By the middle of the fifty-six to sixty-three cycle, however, his ideas were mature enough to be voiced to friends and representatives of the various peace movements. Although he died at the close of this cycle (sixty-three), his wishes were inscribed in the will which formed the basis of the Nobel Peace Foundation. Thus his vast fortune, in a sense the harvest of destruction, was reseeded in the hopeful future of humankind. Although Nobel was truly a son of the Age of Technology, his ideals nonetheless eventually emerged to champion the cherished virtues of the human spirit. In other words, this terrible contradiction engendered the impulse which strove to redeem his life's work.

Sixty-three to Seventy: Drawing the Threads

This seven-year span, the ninth, marks a certain cyclic conclusion, a release from the remorseless drive of destiny as the will's flame begins to withdraw to interior regions to prepare for the approaching expansion across the great divide. This does not mean that the cosmic rhythms cease their faithful beat. These years can offer as a blessing, a grace, the opportunity to complete the tapestry of destiny and pass our contributions to those who follow. This is particularly evident in those souls who are still synchronistically engaged in world destiny.

The lives of Copernicus and Galileo were not only synchronized to external events, but their life spans appear to be synchronized with the "mind at large," the "world-mind." The
question is: Were they *chance* instigators of a new kind of
thinking? Or were they the first among many great souls at that
time to be touched by profound changes taking place below the
surface of human consciousness?

If we accept Plato's approach to the mysterious appearance
of new ideas, we learn that we do not create our thoughts but
rather respond to them, reflect or recollect them, when we are
psychologically and physiologically prepared to receive them.
This would mean that the personal is synchronized to the
transpersonal. Perhaps, then, ideas, like events, have their
proper time too, a time to lie fallow and a time to engage
human interest and involvement. This infers that great ideas,
world-changing ideas, also belong to a universal time organism
and its zeitgeist.

The lives of Copernicus and Galileo reached a certain conclusion at sixty but then completed the finishing touches, so to
speak, between sixty-three and seventy. Copernicus's rather
uneventful life was ruthlessly ruled by a single compelling idea,
that the sun, not the earth, is at the center of our planetary system. This view, taken for granted today, repudiated the old geocentric view of the universe prevalent at that time, a view which
had arisen in the old prescientific prelogical consciousness. By
"removing" the earth from its exalted position, Copernicus
threatened the very sanctuary of knowledge zealously guarded
by the scholastic authority of the Church. Fear of persecution,
therefore, prevented him from publishing his "heretical" bombshell. Eventually, however, he relented to the pressure of his
disciple Rheticus, and the book was published as the seventy-
year-old astronomer-priest lay on his death bed. Little is known
of the personal crises of Nicolaus Copernicus, but there is no
doubt that his personal destiny was poised at the mighty thresh-

old of a new age of human consciousness and prepared the way for such men as Brahe, Galileo, Kepler, Newton, and Descartes. The river of life generally becomes more tranquil as it approaches its outlet, but this is no reason to expect old age to be free of crises. Few of us, however, will suffer the humiliation of Galileo at seventy. Standing on the shoulders of Copernicus, his acute awareness of the physical universe was destined to collide with church dogma. Committed to the study of astronomy, physics, mechanics, and mathematics, Galileo wrote his first book at forty-two and at sixty began work on the "heretical" treatise which affirmed the Copernican image of the heavens. Although ill at sixty-three, he completed it at sixty-six and then went to Rome to seek permission for its publication. The tragic second half of this cycle was dominated by the merciless interrogation of the Inquisition.

It is nearly impossible today to imagine the cataclysm which struck the theological establishment when the frontier minds of that time shifted the earth from its center of celestial glory. This sudden shift in perception and thinking, this urge to explore and observe the physical universe, was a cardinal threshold in the history of human thought, and it turned science and religion into antagonists. The old cosmology and mythological geography were superseded by astronomy and physical geography.

Meanwhile, poor old Galileo, while ill and despondent, was torn to shreds by a conspiracy of obsolete minds resistant to change. Seventy is no time to challenge such dragons, and we can understand why the old fellow, under the threat of torture, bent to the will of the Inquisition. "My error, then, has been—and I confess it—one of vainglorious ambition and of pure ignorance and inadvertence." Despite this tragic setback, however, he continued to work on his great book on mechanics until fate dealt him another cruel blow by taking his sight from him. Although his life ended in rejection and pain, his mind, like Copernicus's, was midwife to the new age of exploration.

The Closing Years

"So the Lord blessed the latter days of Job more than his beginning..." —Job 42:12

"Better is the end than the beginning thereof."

—Ecclesiastes 7:8

Freed from the yoke of ambition and responsibility, released from the hunger of destiny, the elderly have time for themselves. Those who have preserved their mindfulness can at last pick up some of the interests which have long lain fallow. Moreover, they have time to stand and stare, to sense and review their past in a new way. A spry, unwearied soul, still with its sense of expectation, will overcome the natural discomforts of age. If, on the other hand, the closing years offer nothing but hopelessness, the life-sapping feeling of uselessness will inevitably accelerate the decline. Those who cannot help themselves to this precious winter fruit will need help, especially if they carry the problems of their youth unresolved into an old age, which brings its own troubles.

Although we may fear old age and the natural change from responsibility to dependency, the meaning of life remains, and so, to a certain extent, does its creative possibilities. The seventy-seven-year-old is as impelled by the infinite within as the seven-year-old is. This time of life, as valuable to the psyche as any other, deserves far more sympathetic understanding, planning, and guidance than it generally receives. For many, the closing years are bereft of compassion, companionship, and dignity. Therapy for the elderly is greatly overshadowed by our lavish concern for the young, which in effect polarizes the community into camps of young and old, productive and nonproductive, relevant and irrelevant.

What is the reason for this one-sidedness? Perhaps it stems from both our inability to interpret the phenomenon of the human being and our horror of death. Unlike the ancients, who venerated age, the modern, pragmatic person is absolutely confounded by death. This fear of extinction springs from our ignorance of the meaning of life. We have lost our sense of *destination* because we do not understand time and our spiritual continuity. Thus we maneuver our old people into the stagnant backwaters of life to await the heaven of the nihilist: nonexistence.

But a society which isolates its old folk does itself and them a great disservice. This is one reason why modern communities lack balance and cohesion; they are too preoccupied with the bright new flowers of life to notice the mature fruit that follows. Thus the old have to do their best with the scraps of compassion they can find. True, we keep them alive, even beyond their natural time, but they cry out for our understanding and involvement, not our pity. This problem can only worsen as the falling birthrate of the Western world swells the geriatric sector.

What does old age represent? The old offer us the fruit of their time. This is why, in the ancient world, the old were the keepers of mysteries and sacred truths. They are the "graduates" of life, the teachers standing on the high escarpments of their time. This innate grace and wisdom is something which can shine through their dependency and vulnerability if we would but notice. The elderly are pictures of our future. Where they have preserved their faculties, we can sense the emergence of selfhood, the wealth of experience and trials overcome. Where they are senile, we can sense their return to simplicity and innocence; decrepitude itself confronts us with the reality of life and death and heightens our own "sense of path."

Time and toil, the unceasing, unconscious labor for selfhood, has wrought qualities in the old which mature only when the cycles of life have turned. They have planted the seeds, served the shop, lain the bricks, and raised their children. Strange as the idea appears, perhaps we should also value their failures. The "leftovers" of one generation give the following generations something to overcome, something to learn from and transform. In other words, their past offers our present a "resistance" which can sharpen the wakefulness of our ideals. No matter what they have done or left undone, they have in one way or another served their tiny corner of the world's becoming.

The essential value and meaning of old age can be found in its disengagement from the demands of the external world. This stage of life deserves the kind of environment which fosters the activity of contemplation and reflection, a place where memory images can be brought up, relived, and reviewed. This is the way the psyche sustains its sense of continuity—as a preparation for after death. After all, old age is the embryonic phase of the afterlife.

. . . .

In conclusion, looking at the individual as a being of body, soul, and spirit offers us a three-dimensional view of biography, one which gives the time element a vital role. The immense psychological importance of the seven-year cyc
First, they regulate the relationship between the inner metabolism of the soul and the conscious mind's experience of itself. Second, they regulate the "digestion" of experience, the conversion of experience into psychological capacities and faculties. Thus, these cycles lead us deeper into ourselves and out again. Swallowed by time at birth, we are disgorged at death into other dimensions of time—even timelessness. Time is merciful after all! Old age is far more than a chronicle of decline and something to be feared. The self is indestructible and holds all its experience ready for other spirals of advancement after death. It stands to reason that the cycles which influence, sustain, and guide the human soul are totally meaningless if all our

gains in self-development are lost at death. This is a crucial point we will deal with in the last chapter. How can we best understand the nature of a cycle? We have marked the beginning, middle, and end, but we need to sense the whole. One way to imagine the whole process is to look at its organic, its biological qualities. Each seventh year marks a completion and new beginning. We can imagine it as a seed from the fruit of the previous cycle. As the new cycle unfolds so the seed becomes a plant; it is a growing expression of itself. The emphasis begins to change at the midpoint, and the second hemicycle is a phase of internalizing, digesting, absorbing, inhaling the experiences of the first hemicycle. The second half produces the fruit and seed formation. In other words, there is an exhalation-inhalation rhythm behind our changes in consciousness. This is the primary mission of the seven-year cycle.

3

The Chronos Cycle

"The Fates lead him who will, him who won't they drag." —Seneca

Old Chronos-Saturn: the Time Lord

In contrast to the rich vibrato of the seven-year cycle, the thirty-year rhythm sounds a deep basal tone beneath the complex rhythms of the shorter life cycles. One notices a remorseless inevitability about this cycle. I believe it may be the most basic ingredient in the time life of the individual.

Teilhard de Chardin saw life ever consuming life, forever in its becoming, with the cosmos participating in the agony of all things. This picture, in some respects, bears a more than coincidental resemblance to the ancients' mythological notion of Chronos-Saturn, the aboriginal time god who devoured his own offspring. It is as if the grave eminence of old Father Time lives on within our unconscious motivation, using our past to construct our future. If he does, I suspect that he compels us to reap where we have sown and to sow where we have reaped, his inexorable scythe sweeping our present moments into the past, where they scatter as seeds for future harvests. True to his primordial character as the Father of Time, he tells us that we can never escape the tiniest fragment of our past. *In time*, every action is recorded and must be accounted for, since the future inherits the past and must transform it.

The prelogical soul of the ancient sage knew Saturn-Chronos as both the "Lord of Fire" and the grand coordinator of past, present, and future. According to the ancients, the awesome "Lord of Necessity and Cosmic Memory" impels humankind to move toward fulfillment through the spirit-will from which the future—personal, global, and universal—is being ever prepared. Let us then take a closer look at the time role of Chronos-Saturn as our ancestors imagined it.

Many myths have a cosmological meaning. Far from being infantile constructions, cosmological myths are a kind of prescientific astronomy describing the spiritual drama behind the origin of humankind and universe. What is more, the ancients depended on these colossal imaginations to keep their spirit and their terrestrial ambitions in harmony with the never-ending creation of which they were a part and which patterned their codes of conduct. According to archaic spirituality, the exalted figure of Father Time is an essential presence in any creation myth. As "Lord of the Measures," or the "Indicator," *it was he and his kin the "Time Lords,"* who organized the very time structure of our universe.

As we noted in Chapter 1 the mysterious affinity between the time system of the cosmos and the microcosmic time organism of the individual was central to the ancients' way of looking at life. The Spirit of Time was the source of order and destiny. As such, his presence was felt in the humble fate of every soul, and the biography of every soul was written into the eternal cosmography of the universe. It was a truly magnificent conception.

There is no doubt that the Greek-Roman god Chronos-Saturn and the planet of that name spring from the same root. Saturn, says Macrobius (a Latin grammarian of the late fourth and early fifth centuries B.C.) is the "originator of time." The word *Kronos* is derived from the Greek *krounos* meaning "spring" or "source." *Kronos*—or Chronos (time)—ruled the universe until displaced by his son Zeus-Jupiter (wisdom). Of course we should expect the "Time Lords" to appear under many names. Prometheus, the Greek Titan, for example, was a Saturn character insofar as the god Kronos was himself the *Lord of the Titans*. Again, as the "Lord of the Triakontaeris," Saturn governed the thirty-year period of the Persian and Egyptian royal jubilees.

Something of his time character was also stamped on the gods Ptah and Maat in Egypt, Me in Sumer, Parshu in Akkadia and Huang-ti, the yellow Emperor, in China. As king of Italy during its mythological golden age, Saturn was depicted with sickle and ears of corn as the personification of time, governing both agriculture and human cycles. Egyptian priests proclaimed him the universal demiurge who fashioned all the time worlds. As the master smith, he was understandably the celestial patron of artisans, smelters, and master builders. In Babylon, he was the "Planet of the Sun," the "Sun of Night." Likewise, the Indian god Varuna surveyed the first creation and said, "I have fastened the sky to the seat of the Rita." Every mythology has its time god.

The power of Chronos-Saturn set the polycyclic universe aspinning, and I believe there is more to his symbolic time nature than meets the eye. Indeed, the thirty-year rhythm in human biography can reasonably be called the "Saturn Cycle" since the sidereal period of the planet is twenty-nine years and 168 days.

The Thirty-year Phases

The thirty-year cycles are often the most dramatic of all the cycles. This means that our thirtieth and sixtieth years, along with the midpoint at forty-five, are likely to be scored by crucial incidents or a change of pace, direction, and emphasis. There is much evidence to support the view that each climactic predicament typical at these times summarizes the previous cycle and provides the impetus and opportunity for important experiences to come. These are the principal turning points where time and destiny focus on the present. A change of some kind is demanded—an adjustment to jerk us back on course, a course known only to the psychic center of our being.

The three major spans of the Chronos cycle are the formative period, from birth to thirty; the constructive period, from thirty to sixty; and the reflective period, from sixty to death. The first span is called the *formative* period because during these years we integrate and add to our uniqueness all the shaping and modulating forces of our hereditary and environmental backgrounds. Generally speaking, by thirty we have become more or less aware of our own personality and its contradictions. We have, moreover, attempted to make our natural talents our own and now have a rough idea of our goals. Thus, to a certain extent, the preparatory experience between birth and thirty fashions the tools we need for the second thirty years. The *constructive* period is when we pursue our goals and do most of our inner and outer work. This is when we gather a vast array of experience and inject our virtues, gifts, and striving into a world which, in turn, continually deepens and modifies our consciousness and self-understanding. The closing cycle, between sixty and death, is altogether different in both pace and quality, for it is then that all our previous experience is incorporated into that part of us that outlives earthly death. Although we may then appear inflexible and resistant to change, the treasure of experience won in more enthusiastic days remains, transformed into our inner capacities, the very content of the psyche. This particular span, then, in sharp contrast to the outer activity of the previous one, is much more contemplative and inward. That is why I have called it the *reflective* period.

The section in Chapter 2 that discusses the interior change at twenty-eight should help us sense the transitional quality of the years between twenty-eight and thirty. On the one hand, we have the changing disposition of the psyche, on the other, the synchronistic events of the outer world which break into our lives. In countless cases, the change at twenty-eight does not "materialize" on the surface as a visible event of some kind until thirty or thereabout. This transition is seldom comfortable and may be marked by conflict, frustration, disenchantment, and disruption. In many cases, this major turning point offers vitally significant human relationships or an adventure or journey of some kind. Frequently a time of agitation and tension, in some respects it represents our release from the legacies of the first thirty years. It can be a new beginning, a time when we reset the rudder of the soul. Even sickness may be a symptom of this major "rite of passage," a throwing off of the past to accept the future.

Conflict is another key word for this time, either with ourselves, our vocational or social environment, or in our personal relationships. Thirty is a time when our emergent sense of self may lead us into conflict with the outer conditions of our personal life and career. Such tensions stimulate the forces of change and the need for decision. Of course, many of us are unaware of our interior change, and we may have to be prompted to change course by some external intervention—this is where some kind of synchrony may intervene. Whatever its manifestation, it represents the interior movements of the self straining toward its fulfillment through experience.

Generally speaking, being thirty is an unsettling experience and calls for courage and effort. Yet the storms which may come to tear us down should bring about a new and finer reconstruction. This is particularly a time when we might draw strength from Erich Fromm's words, "Creativity requires the courage to let go of certainty," or Hölderlin's: "Where danger is, there is salvation also." In the same spirit, Leonardo da Vinci, a man forever battered by the squalls of fate, said, "He turns not back who is bound to a star." But who is not bound to his or her own star?

The thirtieth-year transition is often a time for self-appraisal. Goethe, for example, demonstrates this perfectly by recording the entrance of his thirtieth year in his diary. We can read that he put his things in order, looked through all his papers, and burnt all the old chips, as they reflected upon other times, other cares. He saw his older writings as the extravagances, impulses, and eager desires of his youth, how he had sought satisfaction in all directions. How he had delighted in mysteries; how he had only half seized hold of science, and let it slip; how shortsighted he was in divine and human things; how many days wasted in sentiments and passions; how little good he had drawn from them. And now that the half of his life was over, he found himself advanced not one step on his way, but standing there as one who having escaped from the waves, begins to dry himself in the sun.

Travel is another archetypal symptom of this turning point. In Winston Churchill's case, it meant crossing the floor of the House of Commons! Twenty-nine and a half on June 30, 1903, the young conservative politician was embroiled in conflict. Churchill struggled with his own indignation and disenchantment as the government of that time, led by Arthur Balfour, was stricken with internal revolt. In a letter of 1903, he confessed that he was an English liberal and that he hated the Tory party, their men, their words, and their methods. He felt no sort of sympathy with them. Against his own inclination, he took a backward step in subscribing to Balfour's policy, though he felt very uncomfortable about what he had said, and at times was not sure even of its honesty. To go on like that, wavering between opposite courses, feigning friendship to a party where no friendship existed, and loyalty to leaders whose downfall was desired, sickened him. Despite venomous attacks for his disloyalty, he joined the ranks of the Liberals on May 31, 1904. It was a major change in direction.

In sharp contrast to Churchill's "journey of political conscience," the longer, more hazardous adventure of the great Carthaginian general, Hannibal (245–183 B.C.), was also a turning point of destiny complete with decisions, anguish, obstacles, and conflict. Hannibal was twenty-nine when he decided to attack the Roman legions on their own ground, an action which he hoped would distract the ever-lengthening arm of Rome from grasping his homeland. The decision to maneuver his armies over the perilous Alps must have weighed heavily on his soul. Only brilliant organization and the trust of his men could have welded such a diverse assemblage of people into a fighting force capable of facing the disciplined armies of Rome. Following the agony of the decision, he had to face the forests, rivers, mountains, autumn snows, and hostile tribes along the way. Despite all this, most of his forty thousand men and forty elephants entered the valley of the Po in November, 218 B.C. The famous battles of Trasimeno and Cannae were a disaster for Rome; at Cannae alone, Rome lost fifty thousand men compared to Hannibal's six thousand. The invincible general went on for fifteen years to terrorize the length and breadth of Italy, striking fear into every Roman heart. Destiny decreed, however, that he would never take Rome. At the mid point of this cycle (forty-five) Hannibal was forced to release his grip on Italy to defend Carthage, which was being threatened by the legions of Scipio. The Carthaginian force was vanquished, but its elusive commander escaped to the east where his legendary shadow continued to haunt Rome for many years. He committed suicide in 183 B.C., moments before the Romans finally caught up with him.

There is no need to multiply these examples, but I will include a brief mention of Alexander von Humboldt, since both the beginning and the ending of his constructive cycle were marked by remarkable journeys. Considered to be the founder of modern geography, Humboldt shone brightly in the constellations of nineteenth century science. Besides his valuable contributions to geophysics, he is especially remembered for his superbly documented exploration of South America. Those who read his biography will easily recognize how experiences in his formative cycle prepared him for his later tasks, and how his early interest in engineering and science generated an irrepressible urge to explore the unknown. He began collecting scientific instruments for his first expedition toward the end of his first thirty-year cycle. Despite several frustrating setbacks, he eventually received permission from the Spanish government and sailed for South America in 1799, only weeks before his thirtieth birthday. This great enterprise was the major turning point in his life. He spent the following thirty years writing a detailed journal of his discoveries, developing his manifold scientific pursuits, and fulfilling his ambassadorial duties. At sixty, thirty years after his first expedition, he set out again, this time eastward into Siberia. During his reflective cycle he produced the magnificent work *Cosmos*, four volumes illustrating the vast complexity of the sciences and their future potential. This brilliant survey, warmed by his sincerity and his reverential approach to everything in the universe, was a splendid synthesis and summation of everything he had learned during his constructive cycle. Indeed, his life was marvelously rounded out.

Before we examine a number of biographical sketches to better observe the phenomena that typify this cycle, I must raise again the serious limitations of trying to evaluate a particular portion of an individual's direction, singularity, and unity. By isolating particular events and their times, we risk depriving ourselves of the full sense of their overall value. Despite this danger, I have chosen to illustrate some of the archetypal phenomena. I hope that the reader will later read some of the biographies in full and thereby perceive the significance of the events in their full context. The handful of lives presented here were selected from a vast number researched in detail, lives which also clearly exhibit the working of this rhythm. Before we look at them, we should also bear in mind that the laws of time in no way impair the spontaneity, potential, and freedom of an individual life; the laws of time are the universals woven into the fabric of the personal. They merely structure our experience.

The Synchrony between Personal and Social Destiny

The social, national, and global movements of humankind, to have any direction, rhyme, or reason, must be a *process*—and as such, manifests itself in Time. The life of the individual is not a closed system but is enmeshed in the intricate time webs of nation and civilization. The tidal motions of civilizations cannot be separated from the humble souls who rise and fall with them. The thirty-year cycle indicates not only a personal point of departure but is also often clearly synchronized to the undertow of change which energizes the social metabolism of humankind. There are distinct focal points of action and reaction where personal destiny appears to engage or disengage itself from national destiny. Obviously, this important factor is particularly noteworthy in the lives of great statesmen. A thorough study lies beyond the scope of this book, but we should at least acknowledge this time mesh between personal and national genesis. Thus we shall first mention briefly a few eminent political figures before paying closer attention to several particularly interesting lives.

Mao Tse-Tung (1893–1976) had just reached his thirty-year transition when he was elected to the Central Committee of the Chinese Communist Party, a point marking his emergence as a significant political figure. By the time he was halfway through the constructive cycle (forty-five), he was in control of the policy and ideology of the party and also embroiled in the bitter struggle against Japan. The conclusion of his cycle (sixty) was synchronized with the death of Stalin. Under Mao's patriarchal hand, Chinese communism separated itself from Moscow and pursued an independent line. Mao's momentous entrance into his reflective cycle is also marked by the formal consecration of the Constitution of the Chinese People's Republic (September 1954) and the inception of China's famous five-year plan.

John Fitzgerald Kennedy stood in his thirtieth year in 1947 when he launched the first phase of his political ascent and was elected to the House of Representatives. Naturally, the destiny of his brother Robert was interlaced with the fortunes of John, whose rapid climb provided the newcomer with invaluable political insight and opportunity. Robert was approaching thirty when he toured the Soviet Union, a "journey of consequence" typical of the Chronos cycle. He described it as a "great adventure" which consolidated his strong anticommunist feelings. More importantly, Robert's transition coincided with John's fight for the nomination for vice president, and the thirty-year-old Robert took charge of marshaling support for his brother. It proved to be the first Kennedy defeat, but the experience would serve them both well in the future. The youngest brother, Edward, was also thirty when he first set foot on the political ladder, and, like Robert, he also made politically motivated journeys at the time to Ireland and Italy. This was when he decided to run for the Democratic nomination to complete the two years of John's unexpired Senate term. So thirty was a political landmark for all three of them. Jacqueline Kennedy, incidentally, was thirty in 1960 when she participated in her husband's race for the presidency and was thirty-one when she became First Lady.

LAWRENCE OF ARABIA

All biographers of T.E. Lawrence (1888–1935), both debunkers and glamorizers, have been captivated by his mystique. Either they love him or they hate him. Never are they indifferent to this enigmatic man who was part ascetic and part warrior, a bewitching brew of archaeologist, soldier, mechanic, diplomat, and prophet. I wish here to draw particular attention to the remarkable turn of his high tide between twenty-eight and thirty. This was the point in his life when his passionate involvement with Arabia reached a critical stage, followed soon after by his disengagement and withdrawal into a private shell.

Indeed, the startling contrast between his first and second cycles makes these climactic years even more noteworthy. In his case, it would be more fitting to use the word "epilogue" than "constructive cycle." For me, this is the most astonishing feature of an altogether astonishing life. His formative cycle and transition seem to contain all his compulsion, urgency, and sense of destination, while his personal destiny was totally saturated by a greater, social destiny. His constructive cycle, on the other hand, shows an abnormal loss of drive, direction, and goals. Once he had made his great contribution, he was left with little save his humble, purely personal pursuits.

The life of Lawrence raises several intriguing questions. Why, for example, was his youth dominated by a compulsive interest in the Crusades? Even as a child and adolescent, he was totally mesmerized by that period of history. His preoccupation with the past nurtured his empathy with the modern Arabian world, but why did the impulse reach a climax around thirty and then pale into insignificance? It was as if some instinct in the depths of his spirit were already committed to the cause.

Apparently, once he had made his offering to it, he was freed to return to his personal destiny. To put it another way, the transpersonal part of his destiny appeared to subside into the personal as he withdrew from that crucial stage of the development of the Middle East.

Looking at his formative cycle, we can sense that future events cast long shadows before them. The structure of his life, moreover, supports the idea that synchronistic events cluster at particular stages of an individual's development. By the time he had reached puberty, he was hooked on the embroilments of the Crusaders and their antagonists. He had explored, mapped, and photographed many of the crusader castles of Europe, absorbing all that he could from their romantic past. Although he took little notice of university life, his sense of separateness was balanced somewhat by his impudent humor and obvious unconventionality. One foot stood among the scholarly, musty libraries of Oxford, while the other yearned for the burning sands of Arabia. Choosing as his thesis "The Influence of the Crusades on the Medieval Architecture of Europe," Lawrence explored the castles of Syria and Palestine, traveling alone and on foot in the heat of summer. With remarkable self-assurance, the twenty-one-year-old seemed to know where he was going. "Men like Lawrence," wrote Robert Payne, "travel only as they will, pitch a tent only as long as they desire, and with every dawn they are in danger of moving on."

Welcoming the dangers of the wasteland, Lawrence tramped all over the Middle East in the years that hatched the First World War. While retracing the old crusader paths, he inhaled the spirit of modern Arabia and became entangled in its politics. This period (twenty-one to twenty-eight) was the time when his destiny meshed with the awakening destiny of Arabia. Perhaps some innate force in his own soul had to be added to the mounting political groundswell. It was as if he were charged to appear at the right place and time; there was something that had to be done, perhaps some ancient wrong to be redeemed or a future to be seeded.

Arabia, at that time, was a volatile mixture of tribes led by chieftains under the eye of the Turkish military. Naturally, when the First World War brought the pot to a boil, the unorganized Arab freedom movement tried to secure British support. Britain, we should remember, sought to prevent capture of the Suez Canal, which was threatened by Turkey's secret agreement with Germany in 1914. Thus the fate of Mesopotamia was suspended between British and Turkish interests.

This, then, was the political canvas upon which Lawrence made his mark. As junior intelligence officer in the British Army map department in Cairo, he became involved in the political intrigues of his countrymen and the Arabs, his adopted brothers. Devoted to the Arab cause and knowing the terrain like an old crusader, Lawrence saw everything through both a European and an Arabian eye. Sharing with Faisal (the future king of Iraq and Syria) the dream of a united Arabian empire, he suddenly found himself in a position to influence the political rapport between Britain and the Arabs. This situation, in a sense, echoed the great historical opportunity which had brought Richard Coeur de Leon and Saladin together during the Crusades of the twelfth century. Was it time for the old and incomplete drama to be reenacted on a modern stage?

Lawrence was twenty-eight when he and his band of marauders harassed the Turkish supply lines by wrecking trains and blowing up bridges. Despite the wounds and humiliations of his escapades, he reveled in the excitement and sense of purpose. He helped direct the famous attack on the old crusader fortress at Akaba, and his prestige grew to the point where he was able to act as the fulcrum between Faisal and Allenby, the British field marshal. The desert campaign ended with the fall of Damascus six weeks before the close of the war. Lawrence was thirty-one.

The peace talks of 1919, upon which depended the future stability of the Middle East, were wrecked by claims and counter-
claims. Lawrence, supporting the claims of Faisal, was highly
suspicious of the French. (Here was yet another echo from the
Crusades, reminding us of the claims of the Frankish knights on
Syria.) Lawrence straightaway made plans for a new campaign,
but other events intervened. The personal side of his destiny had
begun to assert itself, and the transpersonal faded dramatically.

His withdrawal really began when he entered his constructive cycle. He was thirty when his plane crashed on the way
back from his father's funeral. Despite his injuries, he continued his journey to Cairo, beginning on the way the introductory
chapter to *The Seven Pillars of Wisdom*. Not long after the
peace conference, the battered crusader retired to the cloisters
of Oxford, safe in a seven-year scholarship, to complete his history of the desert war. But he found no peace there. In 1919, the
American lecturer Lowell Thomas toured Britain to draw public attention to the desert exploits of the man he cast as a hero of
mythical proportions. This spotlight was more than Lawrence's
highly complex psyche could handle, but it did enable him to
be present at the concluding episode of the Arabian drama. The
inconclusive conference of 1919 had led to the revolts of 1921,
and Lawrence was invited to attend the conference which eventually made Faisal the king of Iraq.

This last thread tied, Lawrence was suddenly left alone.
Drained, disoriented, and near collapse, he tried to reorganize
himself by plunging into obscurity. Indeed, his personal sunset
was almost as rapid as that of his beloved desert sun. Through
his menial service as a mechanic and then as a humble army
private, he sought refuge in a collective body. Unrecognized at
first, the leader became the servant, in a strange way welcoming
the humiliation inflicted upon him for his peculiar habits. Later,
despite the occasional irritations of his fame, he found a measure of contentment in the Royal Air Force. He had always

been intoxicated by speed, whether on land, sea, or in the air. Speed satisfied both his appetite for excitement and his interest in machines. Lawrence, aged forty-seven, was killed in a road accident while riding his powerful motorcycle.

JAWAHARLAL NEHRU

The innumerable threads of meaning which create the time-scape of biography also form the shifting geometry of history. This interdependence is seen in the life of the great statesman, Jawaharlal Nehru (1889–1964). Nehru was born into the elite Brahmin caste and lived the life of a young aristocrat, oblivious to the desperation of the multitude. Educated in Britain in the style of an English gentleman, he was there exposed to those Western values which shaped one side of his political thinking. These formative influences took root in his soul and later, when grafted onto the aspirations of a free India, helped position his nation as the bridge between the political minds of East and West.

Nehru's destiny began to intersect the line of India's emergence as his first thirty-year cycle drew to its close. His thirtieth year "coincided" with profound shifts in Indian consciousness which were about to erupt on the surface. The rising spirit of nationalism was personified in the gentle yet unquenchable flame of Mohandas Gandhi, who soon realized that his young friend Nehru should be groomed for a great task. Although their friendship awakened the disciple's political senses and gave him a mission, Nehru had first to learn to communicate with the masses and to experience the "metabolic" power of the people. As it happened, the 1919 massacre of the Punjab suddenly knocked the twenty-nine-and-a-half-year-old aristocrat off his intellectual pedestal onto the ground of the people. That year also brought him into sharp conflict with his father's more cautious, conservative approach to India's independence.

Nehru's constructive period, which eventually took him to the highest ranks of the Congress Party, India's independence movement, was totally devoted to India's thirty-year struggle for freedom. This was a period of internal dissent, riots, and nine intermittent years in prison. The obstacles were formidable; the deeply rooted caste system, the strife between Hindu and Moslem, and a course to be charted for this ponderous new state. Although the magical rapport between Gandhi and the Indian folk-soul had largely shaped Nehru's outlook, he had the vision to look beyond the internal dilemmas to the role of India in world affairs.

Everything reached a climax in the last two years of his constructive period. First, he had to absorb the terrible loneliness he felt after Gandhi's assassination; then came the exuberant day of dedication and the inauguration of the constitution. The general euphoria was short-lived, however, and his uneasy alliance with Patel had to contend with the social hemorrhage caused by the Pakistan problem and the fissures in Indian society torn open by Gandhi's death. In his sixtieth year, Nehru visited the United States for the first time and addressed the United Nations. Patel died in that same year, and Nehru was elected prime minister to guide his fledgling nation through a series of political, religious, and economic storms. Through his leadership, India established its vital neutrality and became a fulcrum between East and West.

To sum up: at thirty, Nehru discovered his political mission; thirty years later his constructive period closed when the old disciple became leader of an independent India.

JOHANN CHRISTIAN SMUTS

The childhood and adolescence of Johann Christian Smuts (1870–1950) belonged to the homely atmosphere of the South African Cape. His agile and penetrating mind soon attracted attention at Stellenbosch University and he went on to Cambridge, where his tutors forecast a brilliant career in law. After graduating, he returned to his homeland to marry and set up practice. Quick to notice his skills, the government appointed him state attorney of the Transvaal Republic, which at that time stood on the brink of war. Britain severed all diplomatic ties with the intransigent Boer nation in 1899, and hostilities broke out soon afterward. Smuts, at twenty-nine and a half, was made a general in the Boer Army, which was composed of desperate, sharpshooting farmers, who, for a time, held the highly trained British forces at bay. Against great odds, Smuts and his elusive commandos harassed the British war machine.

Thus, at the beginning of his second cycle Smuts was in contact with the men, both friends and foes, with whom he would later negotiate peace and bring a new nation into being. Although the bitter Boer-British conflict engulfed his law career for a time, it also helped forge a mind capable of the discipline, nimbleness, guile, patience, and fairness which together form the art of a great negotiator. His political and personal integrity, respected by both Boer and Briton, put him in the forefront of the settlements which brought the Union of South Africa into being. Moreover, the emphasis of his career shifted in the course of his constructive period from individual to national law, thence to the international field and his contribution to the ill-fated League of Nations. As one of the world's leading statesmen, Smuts signed the Treaty of Versailles, although he did so protesting that it failed to embody his hopes for a just and lasting peace.

Smuts's government was defeated in his sixtieth year, another great turning point. His retirement allowed him time to travel, to pursue his scientific interests, and to write and reflect. From fifty-nine to sixty, this much-respected elder statesman traveled abroad, lecturing on the political trends of the future. Soon afterward, he became the commander-in-chief of his nation during the Second World War. His career reached its grand conclusion when his vast experience and expertise helped pave the way for the formation of the United Nations.

The rich patterning of Smuts's life, barely touched on here, has an impressively organic look about it, its course of development intersecting the destinies of groups and nations at particular times. He himself, I might add, believed that biography, if studied in the right way as a science of "personology," would disclose the laws of evolution behind human nature. In his book, *Holism and Evolution*, he presents the view that his proposed biographical studies would eventually uncover the clearly defined laws of inner growth and development, and that all the different stages and phases were orchestrated by the inner personality. Despite the uniqueness of every personality, all would conform to a general time plan. He suggests that a comparison of these personality curves would reveal the laws of personality and thus bring many of the obscure mysteries of the human life span into the light of understanding.

Conflict, Constriction, Release, and Breakthrough

For many souls the years between twenty-eight and thirty are intensified by stress, turmoil (even conflict), as well as a key event. It could be described as a period of psychic *congestion*, a contraction prior to a burst of expansion; indeed, it is rather a concentrated transition in many lives. This is where the seven and the thirty-year cycles are meshed as both complete their respective tasks before opening an expansive surge of creativity. For many, the span between twenty-one and twenty-eight is teeming with raw experiences. Naturally, all this has to be properly absorbed and digested. There is a subtle though sometimes disconcerting change in self-awareness around twenty-eight which interacts with the completion of the major destiny cycle at thirty. The build-up of psychic pressure is released at thirty, and this often results in a breakthrough into another phase of biographical genesis and fresh opportunity. (See diagram 2.)

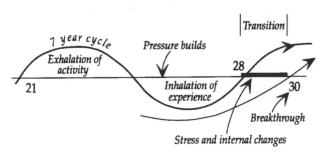

Diagram 2

On many occasions Rudolf Steiner drew attention to highly significant phenomena resulting from a period of repression of the forces of the psyche. He likened it to the squeezing of a rubber ball. The more the compression, the greater the force of expansion when released. This simple example is very relevant to understanding the structure of destiny and its karmic patterns. (We will discuss karma later on.) There are countless examples of souls frustrated by abuse, neglect, and repression in early life. This suffering, however, serves to concentrate the psychic drive for a remarkable and fruitful expansion later on. There is a direct connection between early suffering and the creativity which follows. This is why the pressure between twenty-eight and thirty may well lead to a breakthrough as new cycles are born.

For Mary Ann Evans (1819–1880), the English novelist and literary genius known as George Eliot, the Chronos cycle coincided with points of emphatic and fateful change. Her formative period encased her in a protective religious envelope safe from the world's vanities and distractions while she pursued her evangelical and philosophical studies. Her father, the epitome of the Victorian patriarch, directed and disciplined her first cycle, holding up the finger of religious indignation whenever she was tempted to relax her religious observances. Perhaps her psychological makeup and remarkable intellect needed his restraining and forming masculine force. Whatever the reason, we can imagine the traumatic impact of his death at the end of this cycle (May 30, 1849). "What shall I be without my father?" she wrote as he lay dying. "It will seem as if part of my moral nature were gone. I had a terrible vision of myself last night becoming earthly, sensual and devilish for want of that purifying restraining influence."

With her father's voice hushed, Mary Ann at last broke free. Six days later, she set out for a tour of Europe. Not long afterward, she set Victorian tongues a-wagging when her need for a masculine protector led her to Weimar to "live in sin" with the already married George Henry Lewes, one of Goethe's biographers. Lewes provided the necessary support and love for most of Mary Ann's constructive period. Theirs was one of the most distinguished and lasting love affairs of the nineteenth century. It was during this cycle that her works achieved enormous popularity. Lewes died in November 1878, so in this case the Saturn cycle was very precise, marking clearly defined turning points in her life: she lost her lover twenty-nine-and-a-half years after the death of her father, who died when she was twenty-nine and a half.

The biography of Marilyn Monroe (1926–1962) clearly illustrates her desperate struggle to grasp a self-sustaining identity for herself between twenty-eight and thirty. Her life demonstrates how prolonged and damaging experience in her bleak formative years made it virtually impossible to fulfil her constructive cycle. Her life accentuates the tie between the psychic seven and the broader sweep of the destiny cycle. Marilyn's thirtieth year marks her valiant effort to gain control of her life.

Monroe's childhood was the absolute opposite of George Eliot's, which had more than enough protection, discipline, and continuity. Yet this crucial period of Monroe's life, so bereft of certainty, was the only psychological base supporting a film career which made outrageous demands on her troubled soul. It was a wonder that this semiorphan, bred on instability, was able to achieve anything at all. Her father was unknown to her for many years, her brother was emotionally disturbed, and her mother and grandmother ended up in mental asylums. With so much upheaval (she had twelve foster parents), she failed to develop any lasting sense of commitment and trust. Without roots, she was threatened by every storm. Despite her vulnerability, this lively, intelligent young woman managed to find her way into the movie industry without really trying.

Monroe's rapid climb to stardom as a sex goddess began when she was twenty-one. One can imagine the intense pressures of making one film after another in which she played the dumb blonde. Only a firmly centered individual could have resisted being swallowed by the tinsel dragons of Hollywood. While the moguls manipulated and the public lauded her natural sexuality, her emerging personality had little opportunity for reflection and self-assessment. Thus, with no time to heal the wounds of the past, she was bound to become more and more estranged from herself. This deluge of experience and mounting unease, together with a deeply rooted fear of insanity and death, made a crisis at twenty-eight inevitable. The natural interior change at that time took the form of a desperate attempt to touch her own reality beneath the skin of her exploited sensuality.

During that seven-year cycle she had become a world celebrity, but her fame threatened to suffocate her emerging self-awareness. It was a time for radical change; she needed to do something about her serious psychological predicament. The failure of her second marriage (when she was twenty-eight) and her conflict with Twentieth Century Fox were symptomatic of her turmoil. She felt she must break with the past, cease being a celluloid puppet, and become an actress in her own right. Thus she severed her connections with Fox at twenty-eight. The last movie in this phase was the "*The Seven Year Itch*"!

Monroe was twenty-nine and a half when she left Hollywood to form her own company (Marilyn Monroe Productions), hoping desperately that her life would be less exploited and more self-directed. The thirty-year-old star went to great lengths, taking acting lessons from Lee Strasberg, who had developed methods based on the actor's self-involvement, self-mastery, and self-understanding. This attempt, together with numerous sessions of psychoanalysis, involvement with intellectuals, and her marriage to Arthur Miller, represented an epic struggle to find psychological security. For a while, it looked as if she might succeed; she certainly had more protection, more self-confidence and control.

Despite all this effort, however, Monroe apparently committed suicide at thirty-six. The word "suicide" is rather harsh in this case. It would be more fitting to call her death an "inevitable accident." Her tragedy reminds me very much of Vincent van Gogh's since neither could realize their psychological possibilities between twenty-eight and thirty-five. This meant that the crisis at thirty-five was almost insurmountable, the threshold impassable. As a rule, if one seven-year crisis and its inner opportunities are not grasped, it returns with a vengeance in a later cycle. She, like van Gogh, simply lacked the inner strength; her ego had been weakened by insecurity and by the drugs she swallowed to keep going.

As her precarious grasp on reality slipped, she became increasingly solitary. Her decline during the long battle to complete *The Misfits*, and her return to Hollywood, brought her to the edge of collapse. This abyss was also marked by her feud with Fox over the picture *Something's Got to Give*. Once again, the title tells all. The failure of her childhood, coupled with the success of her film personality, put impossible strains on her psyche. Truly, when the process of individuation breaks down, something's got to give.

Of the hundreds of biographies I have read, that of Honoré de Balzac (1799–1850) is probably the most incomprehensible. One is astonished on the one hand by his peculiar lifestyle and his vain illusions of financial success and worldly fame, and on the other by the depth of human insight and the exceptional industry of immense dimensions.

His was a forlorn childhood deprived of loving care. His father had little involvement and his ill-humored, money-minded mother rejected any display of feeling. "My mother is the cause of all the ill that has befallen me in my life," he wrote later. But it was this deprivation that drove him into the enchanting lair of books. Like so many superfertile souls, hindrance and deprivation served to wind the mainspring of an inner dynamo capable of amazing bursts of energy. There arose within Balzac a ferocious compulsion to etch his name in the world as a man of wealth and esteem.

The ceaseless grind of his formative period, the innumerable potboilers (written under a nom de plume) that flooded French society, served to sharpen the cutting edge of his genius, awaken his powers of observation, and channel his inexhaustible energy. Looking at his life as a whole, all this had to be endured before he could take on the limitless task of recording the temper and diversity of the life and soul of France (*Comedie humaine*).

But what a mess he got himself into at the end of his first thirty-year cycle! Crushed by financial woes, numerous business ventures that backfired, and extravagant snatches at romance, he found, for all his sweat, not a crumb of financial relief or literary fame. All his vitality and optimism moved him not an inch nearer his worldly goals, but they did line the shelves of his experience and imprint themselves on his later work. Stefan Zweig, in his memorable biography of Balzac, highlights this formidable transition. Balzac, despite all his incredible efforts, was absolutely bankrupt as a publisher, as a printer, and as an owner of a type foundry. He was twenty-nine years old and owed one hundred thousand francs. He had worked incessantly for ten years, accepting every kind of humiliation. He had spent his time writing thousands of pages under pseudonyms or fleeing from his creditors. Zweig, however, notes that Balzac earned himself a different kind of treasure. He was compelled to perceive the real dramas of life by *experiencing them*. Thus he could faithfully portray the reality of his own times. Balzac's path of failure, in fact, led him to his artistic triumph.The thirtieth year, therefore, marked the nadir of Balzac's despair but also launched his ascent to fame.

In March 1829, aged twenty-nine years and eight months, Balzac published *Le Dernier Chouan*. This stroke of good fortune lifted his spirit and triggered another frenzy of energy brilliantly converted into productivity. Zweig, noting this remarkable expansion, writes: "Balzac's output in the two years, 1830 and 1831, after his name had begun to have a certain value, is almost unparalleled in the annals of literature."- Balzac produced a stream of novelettes, stories, newspaper articles, and political commentaries which amounted to the equivalent of sixteen printed pages a day. Thus, after ten painful years, Balzac discovered himself as the historian of his age.

Balzac's life clearly illustrates the dynamic contraction and expansion at the end of the formative period and the beginning of the constructive period. His thirtieth year was a point of constriction, frustration, and blockage. But suddenly, something gave way and life and fortune surged forward again. This is typical of the character of the Chronos cycle.

Ralph Waldo Emerson's nature and the general appearance of his life (1803–1882) stand in sharp contrast to the intense character of Balzac's. Nevertheless, we again find the thirtieth year a point of radical change and crisis. Toward the end of his formative period, as Emerson's life began to solidify around him, his creative spirit was forced to struggle for its expansion and liberation from the past. His early development, shaped by the religious currents in Boston and Concord, gently eased him toward a career in the church. For the most part, everything during this relatively untroubled cycle seemed to fall in place quite naturally. He graduated, taught a little, married, and then, as expected, took his place in the pulpit. Then, just when the pattern of his life looked set, Emerson's gentle soul was attacked by pain and doubt. Not only did he have to withstand the death of his young wife after only eighteen months of marriage, but he also found himself more and more at odds with the dogmas of his church as he outgrew its old and lifeless forms of thinking. Emerson increasingly found the pulpit to be the battleground of his conscience.

Realizing that the rift between his emerging convictions and the church was irreconcilable, Emerson announced his resignation. His thirtieth birthday was only a few weeks away. His journal quoted Martin Luther: "It is neither safe nor prudent to do aught against conscience. Here stand I, I cannot do otherwise." And in a letter to his brother he wrote, "The severing of our strained cord that bound me to the church is a mutual relief. It is sorrowful to me and to them in a measure for we are both suited and hoped to be mutually useful. But though it will occasion me perhaps some, (possibly, much), temporary embarrassment yet I walk firmly toward a peace and a freedom which I plainly see before me albeit afar."

Breaking with the past, Emerson in his farewell sermon attacked the traditional formalism of institutions. He then set sail for Europe, "to find affinities between me and my fellows." The continent at that time was seething with kindred souls struggling to free themselves from the grip of archaic institutions, and it offered him plenty of new ideas and personal contacts. His meeting with Thomas Carlyle marked the beginning of a mutually creative friendship which lasted their lifetimes. By the time he returned to America, Emerson felt that his inner problems had resolved themselves. Refreshed in soul and confident of his spiritual path, he was now prepared to discover and then offer the New World a dogma-free approach to an individual-centered morality. Emerson's thirty-year crisis cut him free from his past. His constructive period was relatively free from crisis, and his life progressed in a harmonious way—again, in sharp contrast to Balzac.

The Origin of Species erupted into the intellectual landscape of the nineteenth century and sent shock waves into every nook and cranny of the natural sciences. Through his work, Charles Darwin (1809–1882), as it were, indirectly injected his cold scientific materialism into the warm blood of Creation. In short, his interpretation of evolution led to what amounts to a profane view of nature and humanity as opposed to the sacred, although Darwin himself was deeply religious. The fuse of this bombshell led all the way back to Darwin's thirtieth year.

Darwin's formative period, as we saw in Chapter 2, included the never-to-be-forgotten voyage of exploration which provided the initial surge of inspiration behind his work in the constructive period. As the formative period approached its conclusion, he decided to collect data relevant to his inquiry into the origin of species. The flash of synchronicity which pierced the veil and fixed his future course was his perusal of an essay on population by Malthus, read when he was twenty-nine years and nine months old. In his autobiography, he noted that on October 1, 1838, he happened to read, for amusement, Malthus on population. Darwin's countless observations of plants and animals had primed him to recognize the struggle for existence. It suddenly struck him that favorable variations in an organism's constitution would tend to be preserved, while unfavorable ones would be eliminated. The result would mean the formation of a new species. "Here, then, I had at last got a theory by which to work." The timing was perfect. As Pascal said, "Chance favors the prepared mind," although the word "chance" is inappropriate if the principle of synchronicity was a factor. The thirty-year-old Darwin also suffered from ill health, and he himself noted a distinct alteration in his personality, "this curious and lamentable loss of the higher aesthetic taste." He felt that his mind was being constrained and limited to the production of general laws. Darwin proceeded to work out these laws during the constructive period, *Origin* being first published when he was fifty-one, after years of meticulous research and synthesis. *The Descent of Man*, written between fifty-nine and sixty-three, was the crowning result of the thirty-year labor which had carried him from the origins of nature to the origin and evolution of man.

For many people, the painful experiences in the formative cycle are a preparation for the obstacles awaiting them in the constructive cycle. In the case of Marie Curie (1867–1934), her early experiences of anguish, loss, and sacrifice fashioned the inner resources and stamina needed to survive the demands and disasters of her later life. Born in Poland, Marie was the youngest of five bright children in a happy and closely knit family receptive to learning in general and to the sciences in particular. She was eight when her sister died of typhus. Her much-loved mother, weakened by grief, fell to tuberculosis shortly after. Later, Marie left Poland and her beloved family to work as a governess to support her sister through the university. It was a period of intense loneliness, but her turn came and she graduated from the Sorbonne to embark on a career in science.

The constructive period opened with a crucial decision. She was thirty when she and her husband Pierre became fascinated by the mysterious radiation emitted by radioactive salts. They decided to attempt to isolate the unknown substance responsible for the radiation given off by pitchblende. Sharing a common purpose founded on their love, Marie provided the inexhaustible energy and laboratory competence, Pierre the guiding intellect and vision. After several painstaking years of labor and sacrifice, they succeeded in trapping a precious decigram of the new element which they named "radium." Their personal triumph was rewarded with the Nobel Prize, but sadly, Pierre's tragic death stopped them from savoring their victory and the enormous international acclaim that followed. The loss of her beloved husband and scientific collaborator was a terrible blow.

After a brief withdrawal from the laboratory, Marie mustered the courage to tackle the practical application of radium and to support the cause of international science. During her constructive period, she pioneered the development of X-ray equipment which added a completely new dimension to medical diagnosis and therapy. Looking at her life as a whole, it is doubtful that her career could have survived the inestimable anguish of Pierre's death had she not suffered what one might reasonably call, the "preparatory pain" of her formative period.

Johannes Kepler's brilliant discoveries, namely the laws governing the orbital movements of the planets around the sun, were undoubtedly the links which fastened the central sun of Copernicus to the later work of Newton and his laws of gravity. Born in Weil, Germany, Kepler (1571–1630) viewed his parents as less than ideal. "My father was a man vicious, inflexible, quarrelsome and doomed to a bad end," he wrote. His mother he described as "small, thin, swarthy, gossiping and quarrelsome, of a bad disposition." Little in his childhood and youth softened the squalor of his existence, his extremely poor health, and his erratic education. Susceptibility to illness, together with incessant self-criticism and almost perpetual anxiety, followed him all his life. There were, however, two auspicious events which did set his young soul alight—the comet of 1577 in his seventh year and an eclipse of the moon in his ninth year. These celestial incidents helped shape his decision to study mathematics and astronomy.

Kepler set his sights on unraveling the laws of planetary motion, but his strategy, though brilliant, was impeded by his inability to make accurate measurements. His calculations were distorted by primitive instruments. Yet reliable observations were being recorded at that very time by the flamboyant genius, Tycho Brahe. Destiny therefore conspired to bring them together, and the arc of synchronicity was struck between these singularly dissimilar characters when Kepler's work won Brahe's approval and an invitation to join the master of observational astronomy. Thus Kepler, in his thirtieth year, became Tycho's assistant in Prague and began the analysis of his master's precise measurements of the movements of Mars. Their short-lived collaboration, beset by heated quarrels and suspicion, nevertheless ignited an explosion in the understanding of celestial mechanics. Kepler left the exotic household of the silver-nosed eccentric while he was still thirty, but he had more than enough accurate information to deduce the laws behind the motions of Mars.

The thirty-year cycle of Sir Isaac Newton (1642–1727) is clearly associated with the theme of *conflict* rather than a breakthrough of ideas, which belongs to the twelve-year cycle. It all began in his thirtieth year when he was invited to join the prestigious Royal Society following his astounding discoveries in optics and gravitation at twenty-four (see Chapter 4). His election also marked the beginning of his thirty-year wrangle with Robert Hooke (who, incidentally, produced his own great work, *Micrographia*, when he was thirty). A brilliant inventor and energetic scientist in many fields, Hooke was sanguine, versatile, gregarious, and pragmatic. Newton, in sharp contrast, was solitary and concentrated, his mind revolving around his devotion to the God of universal order. Thus, the antagonism was more than a clash of temperament and pride; it was a collision of consciousnesses.

The mainstay of the Royal Society for forty years, Hooke epitomized the traditional Baconian mind which fluttered here and there searching for discoveries in as many fields as possible. Newton, on the other hand, searched for the fundamental law which would give humanity knowledge of the cohesive unity of the universe. His life's work, as he saw it, was to combat atheism; his industry was not with a design of bidding defiance to the Creator but to enforce and demonstrate the power and superidentity of a supreme being. The thirty-year war between these contrasting scientific styles reached a climax halfway through Newton's cycle (age forty-five) when he published his great work *Principia*. Hooke bitterly accused him of plagiarizing his own findings. The vortex of this dispute, fed by Newtons's almost paranoic fear of criticism, soon sucked in most of the elite of English science.

But Newton's star rose as Hooke's fell, although he would have nothing to do with the society while his adversary lived. The impasse was finally broken by Hooke's death in 1703, when Newton was sixty. At last the king of English science felt free to take control of the society, reforming it in his own image and reigning with absolute authority until his own death in 1727.

In his book *Memoirs of Childhood*, Albert Schweitzer (1875–1965) recalls a momentous decision, one that offers us an excellent example of the connection between the seven-year-cycle and the thirty-year cycle. He tells us that the decision was made when he was twenty-one to dedicate himself to the ministry, to science, and to music until he was thirty. By that time he hoped to have fulfilled himself in both science and music, and would thenceforth follow a path of service "as man to my fellow man". Most people have a vague and hopeful sense of destiny, but few twenty-one-year-olds can plan or predict their course with more than a sniff of certainty. Schweitzer, however, not only had an unusually acute sense of path, he was abundantly blessed by the upbringing, natural talents, and unshakable spiritual confidence to pursue it. Werner Pict, in his book *The Life and Thought of Albert Schweitzer*, mentions Albert's remarkable ability to plan his future course. Pict saw Schweitzer as one of those rare souls who possess a character and a constitution suited to maintaining a continuity with the past. The powerful formative experiences in Schweitzer's past always made their presence felt in the metabolism of his present.

The exceptional caliber of Schweitzer's mind showed itself in his student years when he studied the development of early Christianity. Besides his scholarly and original work on the historical Jesus and Paul, he made his presence felt in the world of music where, under the tutelage of Charles Widor, the organist and composer, he became one of Europe's foremost organists and interpreters of Bach. His intuitive grasp of Bach's work led to a major book on the subject, published when he was thirty. Thus, his formative period, enriched by music, theology, philosophy, and the ministry, placed the world at his feet.

It was a perfect time for the flash of synchronicity which occurred in the autumn of 1904 when he was about twenty-nine and a half. Casually glancing through the *Parisian Missionary Monthly*, his imagination was fired by an article, "The Needs of the Congo Mission," which outlined the dreadful plight of the peoples of the Congo condemned to untreated suffering and disease. His psychological preparedness and a particular external circumstance were fused in that moment of meaning. He knew what he had to do. This was how he should serve.

At thirty, this Doctor of Music, Theology, and Philosophy was ready for his renunciation. Schweitzer knew that he had the health, practical sense, energy, and persistence to transform his idea into reality. Only after he had decided all this did the letters go out informing his friends and relatives of his decision. So he began the arduous business of studying medicine at the university where he had hitherto won renown as a lecturer! This decision was made against the advice of his friends. The last thing he should do, they said, was to bury his genius in the Dark Continent. But Schweitzer was an indomitable rebel. Seven years later, he was poised to give his life to the suffering African. Empowered by his love of service, all his attributes—his versatility, sound health, and uncommon common sense, his musical and philosophical interests—were engaged in his immensely productive constructive period. His global fame allowed him to express his deep concern about the drift of modern civilization toward a depersonalized and desacralized quality of life. Yes, there is something very symmetrical, orderly, and robustly consequential about his life. One is not surprised that he lived out all three terms of his thirty-year cycles, dying when he was ninety.

The emergence of Martin Luther King (1924–1968) from the embittered mass of black America illumines the mysterious process which fashions individuality out of the spirit of the time, the intrinsic nature of the self, and the shaping experiences of the first thirty years. King's destiny, particularly his transition and constructive period, was synchronized with the fermenting discontent bubbling beneath the crust of American consciousness. As his formative period neared its close, his emerging dreams demanded a practical mission for the following cycle.

The son of a Baptist minister in a small town near Atlanta, his religious growth and his collisions with racial hatred and injustice aroused his vision of brotherhood, his moral vigor, and his will to action. A spiritual cousin of Tolstoy and Gandhi, he drew the Sermon on the Mount in general and the principles of nonviolent change in particular, deep into his aspiration. His quest became clear. He must lend his weight to the dispersed and clumsy efforts of the embryonic human rights movement. The magnetic clamor and excitement of those hazardous protests, especially the one in Montgomery, drew the young pastor toward a rubicon of personal reassessment to digest his past and to confirm his ideals and future action. This happened when late in his thirtieth year he was seriously injured by a black woman who stabbed him close to the heart while he was signing autographs in a New York department store. This violent intrusion stood at the very core of his transition. Coretta King, in her book, *My Life with Martin Luther King*, recognized the import of this interruption. She compared her husband's crucial need for quietude and contemplation with the imprisonment of Gandhi and Nehru. "The pressures and hurry and strain were in abeyance, and he could think of his philosophy and his goals, and assess his personal qualifications, his attributes and beliefs."

Before his return to the hustle and bustle of the cause, King made his archetypal journey (aged nearly thirty) when he took up Nehru's invitation to visit India. His perceptions of the well-tested Indian experience of civil disobedience and his meeting with Nehru, himself a disciple of Gandhi, confirmed his conviction that the road of social awakening lay in the direction of political action. Soon after his return to America, he resigned from his church to give himself totally to his future.

In his second cycle, King became the spiritual dynamo behind the black liberation movement. Despite mounting threats of physical danger, the momentum grew day by day. His primary mission as he saw it was to help channel the waking black passion into a nationally regenerative force. He firmly believed, despite the militant factions around him, that the healthy transformation of individuals and nations could be achieved through the power of reconciliation, moral awareness, and Christian action. His leadership not only broadened the vision of American destiny but also refined the techniques of protest, such as sit-ins and orderly marches. Political results were only a matter of time under this sustained pressure.

King's drive against the tyranny of obsolete and obstinate racism made him an international figure and brought him the Nobel Peace Prize. At the fulcrum of his conviction and concentration stood the belief that only morally redemptive suffering could heal the wounds of individuals and nations. But as his light intensified, the shadows grew ever more menacing. An assassin's bullet cut him down when he was thirty-nine, but it was too late—the torch of racial equality was now in full flame.

Cycles of Perfection

After drawing the time charts of hundreds of individuals from luminaries to lesser lights, I have become particularly interested in examples of misalignments. In some lives the time forms are out of synchrony with the planetary rhythms. We could consider this a form of tragedy, since being in the right place at the wrong time and vise versa is a tragedy—a deformed destiny. Life connections cannot be made, gifts remain unused, faculties unexercised, experience unexperienced; and the butterfly remains trapped in the pupa. I will examine this in volume 2, but I mention it here to emphasize the contrast between these unfortunate souls and the great ones, the spiritual guides, the initiates, especially the fulfiller of all the cycles of heaven and earth—Christ Jesus. The more advanced the being, the more their time life, their preparation and mission, both confirms and affirms the spiritual laws working in time. We should therefore expect to find graphic and telling examples of the great transition at thirty. The mythological, cosmological, and historical aspects of these sublime personalities should also be in perfect mesh with the biographical. Every incident along their paths should have occurred at the ordained place and time. Where else, if not in these inimitable journeys, will we find the time harmony of the heavens so perfectly reflected in the veiled pulse of biographical time?

Zarathustra, spiritual leader of the Persians and founder of Zoroastrianism, lived between 660 and 583 B.C. During that time, the *Zend Avesta* was written in its present form. According to legend, Zarathustra was twenty or twenty-one when he left home to seek the man most in love with right conduct and most given to the feeding of the poor. For seven years, Zarathustra remained in silent meditation in a cavern decorated with the image of the world. At the age of thirty, he received certain revelations from the archangels and began the prophetic mission which resulted in conversions stretching as far as Greece and India.

Mahavira (which means "Great Man") was a contemporary of the Buddha and founder of Jainism in the seventh century B.C. His teaching eventually spread to Northern India, the area between the Himalayas and the Ganges. Legend has it, that the great gods themselves presided over his birth. He lived a worldly, luxurious life for *thirty years* until his parents died and the gods reappeared before him, charging him to "propagate the religion which is a blessing to all creatures of the world." Mahavira then gave all his riches to the poor and accepted the ascetic practices of the wandering monks, suffering for twelve years the austerity and temptations which prepared him for enlightenment. At forty-two, he was ready to teach the doctrine of salvation to those who sought deliverance from the dreary round of repeated earth lives. After he had taught for *thirty years*, the gods returned to his side to accompany his triumphant ascent into Nirvana.

Tradition tells us that many wondrous dreams and auguries forecast an immense destiny for Prince Siddhartha. The prince was twelve years old when a council of Brahmins decreed that he would be compelled to devote his life to asceticism if ever he beheld the spectacle of old age, sickness, or death. With this warning in mind, the king installed his son in a sumptuous, secluded palace where he was groomed for his earthly throne. But despite all precautions, Prince Siddhartha did indeed behold the suffering of humanity. Rejecting all his earthly treasures, including his beautiful wife, he entered the sorrow-strewn world in search of enlightenment through meditation and self-denial. The great renunciation, the "Night of the Great Going Forth," took place in his *thirtieth year*. Six years later, Siddhartha reached the summit of his self-transformation under the Bo tree, thus attaining the rank of Buddhahood. The Lord Buddha, (the Awakened One), then set forth on his mission teaching the Eternal Dharma—the middle way between self-indulgence and self-torture.

The Great Magi, those Initiates versed in the star wisdom of antiquity, recognized in the rhythms of Saturn and Jupiter the impending appearance of the new Light of the World. But apart from the Nativity and the temple episode at twelve, little has been recorded of Jesus' formative period until it ended with the thirtieth year. Taking a cosmological viewpoint, Saturn would have returned to the position it held at the Bethlehem birth when Jesus was *thirty*. This second Nativity, so to speak, marked the mighty turning point when the personality of the Christ, through the mediation of John the Baptist, entered the mortal nature of the man Jesus and bestowed on him his spiritual mission. Saturn, incidentally, then stood in the zodiacal sign of Gemini (the Twins). This was the celestial sign informing the expectant, yet blind and deaf world that He who is not of this world had become the divine brother of man.

According to the old myths, Saturn was the great overseer of all the cosmic cycles. Remember, it was he who established the time order of the heavens and the earth. In some respects, old Chronos-Saturn can be said to represent the Father Spirit of our universe. Did the heavens not announce the turning point of the world, the moment of incarnation, by proclaiming, "This is My

beloved Son, in whom I am well pleased?" According to esoteric Christianity, this unparalleled event, this transition of all
transitions, signaled the entrance of the divine into human
nature, the moment when the *Christos*, the *Logos*, the Word,
united with Jesus of Nazareth and entered the stream of human
evolution.

After His baptism at thirty, Christ suffered the temptations
and then began healing and teaching. Yet only three epochal
years separated His baptism from His crucifixion and Resurrection—a mere one-tenth of the usual constructive period. Thus,
his entire cycle was compressed into three immensely dynamic
years. Could it be that the three phases of His life, i.e., Baptism,
Healing-Teaching, Crucifixion-Resurrection, and Pentecost are
archetypes of the biographical process within every human destiny? Although the sequence of Gospel accounts seems far
removed from our ordinary lives, His monumental and paradig-
matic transition at thirty is reflected, albeit on lower octaves, in
every human biography.

When the Christ stepped into the stream of mortal time, He
also accepted the rhythms and cycles which shape all biography. He came to uphold, not reject, the Law. No matter how we
interpret His character and spiritual significance, our lives have
something in common with His. The constructive period, as I
have tried to show in this chapter, is the period in which we
pour into the world all that we have to offer. No one would dis-
agree that we also encounter our own forms of temptation and
even our own ingenious varieties of crucifixion. This is nothing
less than the way to self-emergence. One can only have faith
that our enigmatic and diverse paths of becoming will eventually lead us to higher levels of freedom and deliverance from
Time—which is nothing less than a personal resurrection.

4

The
Jupiter
Cycle

"And there appeared a great wonder in heaven, a
woman clothed with the Sun and the Moon under her
feet, and upon her head a crown of twelve stars."
　　　　　　　　　　　　　　　　—Revelation 12:1

Time and time again while drawing up biographical charts, I
detect the presence of another cycle with qualities quite unlike
those of the seven-year rhythm. The seven regulates the cyclic
patterns of our inward descent through the psychological layers of the personality, but the twelve-year cycle translates this
changing self-awareness into the sequential steps of our life's
work, the psyche's *expression* in the world. Best described as a
vocational rhythm, the twelfth years mark phases of scientific,
artistic, or philosophical activity, the maturing of ideas, spans
of personal relationship, and even the strokes of good fortune
that punctuate our path through life. These are moments when
"something clicks," something meets us just at the right
moment, or a new idea or plan suddenly slips into place. Being
a rhythm of creativity, it is particularly strong in the lives of

creative people. A brief detour into the rich time symbolism of the twelve, and its appearance in mythology and cosmology, will help us appreciate its biographical significance.

The Old Cosmos

The stars which have guided us over ocean and desert for thousands of years now guide our amazing technology to the moon and planets. Yet our modern science of navigation is but a pale metaphor of the celestial guidance ancient people once felt shepherding their destiny. Somewhere along the way, they divided the cosmos into twelve sectors of influence. Imagine how ancient people felt about their universe! Through their mythical and symbiotic connection to the heavens, they felt the stars shaping the geometry of their bodies and throbbing within their destiny. Every civilization had its sacred stories of the unfolding of the cosmos. Not yet children of earth, they saw themselves as children of the sky. It is not surprising that the Bushwomen of the Kalahari hold their newborn babes up to the stars as a token of their gratitude.

But as human beings "fell" toward the isolation of selfhood, toward the experience of themselves as independent selves, the living, intelligence-filled cosmos receded further and further behind veils of speculation. The universe was no longer *experienced*—it was observed. Modern scientists have achieved a complex mathematical rapport with the stars, based on staggering measures of energy, time, and distance. In so doing, they have uncovered the anonymous face of a reality which appears to be oblivious of the human condition. All we perceive now is a derelict, yet still faithfully ticking, cosmic clock vacated by its creators.

Let us compare the stark concepts of modern science with the life-filled, holistic universe of the ancient. One pre-Copernican view imagined a central earth sheathed by concentric planetary spheres bounded by the crystalline sphere of the fixed stars and the empyrean void of timelessness. Such geocentric systems had personal meaning for our forefathers, the builders of the Giza Pyramid, Stonehenge, and the like, when they experienced themselves at the throbbing focus of cosmic life. For them, the planetary "staircase" was the track along which souls descended to be born and ascended after death. The old view pictured pre-birth, life, death, and after death as a continuum inseparable from the all-embracing interest of the cosmos. The sun-centered system which ridiculed all this glory is a product of reason and observation arising from a very different consciousness. The prescientific picture arose from spiritual perception, whereas the current approach is a mathematical one.

The highly calendric life, astrogeometry, and myths of the old cultures all suggest that the ancients saw themselves as members of the dynamic unity of heaven and earth, and this is where the twelve comes in. They believed that this unity was expressed as a twelvefoldness. The *zodiakos*, meaning "circle of signs," is the encircling girdle of star groups through which the sun and planets appear to move in the course of the year. By using our imagination, we can extend the plane of the earth's equator outward until it touches the great celestial sphere. (See diagram 3 on the following page.) Thus we can imagine ourselves standing at the focus of a colossal bubble which appears to rotate together with the zodiacal belt as the earth spins on its axis. The sages of prehistory used this vast cosmic frame as the basis of all their time systems. By dividing the zodiac into twelve, they gave the heavens a time reference—year, month, and so on. *Thus, the twelve was adopted as a frame of reference to connect time and space.*

The cosmogonic myths (star stories) picture the involvement of the cosmos in the destiny of earth and humankind. Much later, Plato imagined the twelve signs as twelve emanations of

the creative force governing and maintaining the functions of
the universe. Even as late as Aristotle, we find that the stars
were regarded as gods. In a letter to his famous pupil Alexander
the Great, Aristotle wrote, "Heaven is full of gods to whom we
give the names of the stars." Indeed, the wealth of anthropolog-
ical and mythological evidence suggests that heavenly powers
were considered responsible for organizing the structure of the
physical world and for preparing the evolutionary path of
human consciousness.

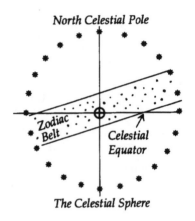

The Celestial Sphere

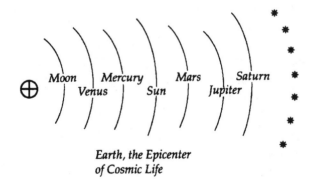

Earth, the Epicenter
of Cosmic Life

Diagram 3

In the Greek and Egyptian mystery religions, the "Harmony of the Spheres" resounded in the symphony of the living world. Famed for their star wisdom, the Chaldeans called the planets "interpreters." The influence of a zodiac sign was interpreted or modified when a planet moved through it. By measuring movement, position, and cycle, the Chaldeans interpreted these correspondences as expressions of cosmic meaning— the "writing of the gods." Indeed, the secretive, esoteric star knowledge taught in the Temple Mysteries of Persia, Chaldea, and Egypt expressed the view that the gods who brought reality into being also prepared the physical ground of our mortal life long before the miracle of personal birth. These gods, moreover, received the fruits of the human being's earthly labors after death, when self and cosmos were reunited. The ancients had a strong sense of destination and divine support. They had the whole universe to hang on to, while we have only ourselves.

The myths, as we saw in Chapter 3, tell us that the establishment of the time order of the world was one of the primary missions of gods, especially Chronos-Saturn, who set the cosmic clock a-ticking, the Norse "World Mill" a-turning. But every individual time organism is an integral part of the universal time-matrix. At the moment of birth, every baby lies at the center of a particular configuration of stars and planets. From time to time in our lives, the planets return to their "original" positions. In this sense, biography represents a kind of *individualized planetary clock*. Of course, all this is totally irrelevant if we insist that the universe is sublimely disinterested in our affairs. But what if the ancients were correct? What if the essence of the self descends through these planetary spheres on its way to the womb? Not only would the cosmos regain its personal meaning and glory, but our prenatal adventures could continue to reverberate in the psyche during our earthly sojourn. In other words, the cyclic activity of the cosmos would manifest itself in biographical time since it is a part of our time organism.

Rudolf Steiner stressed his view that the ancients' dream-like mentality actually *experienced* the rapport between the beings of earth and the beings of heaven. The ancient star wisdom of the Magi which viewed a universe teeming with spiritual activity and evolutionary meaning slowly decayed, or to be more accurate, became transformed by the march of consciousness into our present-day astronomy. As Rudolf Steiner points out: "The kind of knowledge represented by the wisdom of the Magi from the East, has become abstract. The faculty of outward perception expressed in the imaginative, instinctive knowledge of the world of stars and its secrets, in the ancient astronomy which also reckoned with numbers and —to use the platonic term—geometrized with figures, this form of perception which saw a living mathematics being fulfilled in the cosmos and to which every star was a spiritual reality has gone the opposite way. The external perception of olden times withdrew inwards, into the human being, and became abstract mathematics, abstract mechanics or phoronomy—the mathematical-mechanistic knowledge that arises from within us."

Freedom, as we know it, was not then a matter for consideration, since this inclination still lay dormant in the deeps of the psyche. Indeed, the old cosmos was strictly dictatorial, watching over the emerging of human consciousness with a stern gaze and iron hand. In sharp contrast, the enlightened forms of star wisdom emerging today have rejected this old tyranny. The free person is no longer a puppet of the stars, although his development is still anchored in cosmic law and its orders of time. In contrast to the old gods of wrath, the new universe is seen to be compassionate and love-powered, anticipating in future cycles the joyful reunion of the conscious self with itself in freedom. Presumably, we had to outgrow the old cosmos to uncover our own authentic reality. We now seek a creative reunion through our own independent intelligence and will. If this is so, then our reaching for the stars is not a problem of rocket propulsion but rather a pilgrimage into our own interior universe.

"The Church of Israel complains to God: 'Lord of the World, even when a man takes a second wife he thinks of the first; but thou hast utterly forgotten me.' But God answered, 'Daughter, I have 12 mazaloth [signs of the zodiac], and to each massal 30 chel [commanders], and to each chel 30 legions [generals], and to each legion 30 rabaton [officers], and to each rabaton 30 karton [captains], and to each karton 30 kistra [camps], and to each kistron I have assigned 3,650,000,000 stars. All these have I created for thy sake, and yet thou sayest I have forgotten thee."[1]

The creation myths tell of cosmic history, describing with matchless pictorial imagery how one order of spiritual powers was superseded by another. As one hierarchy (Greek: *heiras*, sacred, *archio*, to organize) left the celestial stage, another entered to inject fresh impulses into evolution, and a new age dawned.

Iranian myths relate how the Ancient Father, Zervan Akarna (Unbounded Time), gave birth to the conflicting duality— Ahura Mazda (light) and Ahriman (darkness). This theme of conflict is fundamental to all the myths. For example, the antagonism between the "obsolete" and the new orders of gods at the onset of a new world age can be seen in the myths of the twelve Norse Aesir vanquishing the Jotuns, and the Indian Devas conquering the Asuras. Likewise, in Sumerian mythology we find the sun hero Marduk rejecting Apsu and Tiamat, the keeper of the Tablet of Destinies. Here the twelve is again conspicuous. Apsu and the mother dragon Tiamat begot the gods, but their quarrelsome children rebelled against them. After Apsu was cut to pieces, the furious Tiamat created eleven other gods of

---

1. Interpretation according to R. Rish Lakish, Isaiah XLIX: 14, found in Bab. Baerachoth. (32).

demonic force to support her against the father-killers. These new gods were destined to provide the names of the zodiac signs. The rebels, led by Marduk, overcame Tiamat, took the Tablet of Destinies and transfixed their opponents to the zodiac. This particular myth is a marvelous example of the rise of the planetary gods and "banishment" of the older gods to the periphery of the universe.

I believe the most revealing examples of cosmic conflict and change involving the twelve can be found in the Greek myths. They tell of Chronos-Saturn, the youngest of the twelve mighty Titans, overcoming the previous generation of gods represented by Gaia, the Cosmic Mother, who bore the first race of gods, and by Uranus, the starlit sky. From the Chronos generation came the Fates, the Golden Apples of Immortality, sleep and her retinue of dreams, doom, old age, nemesis, and much else belonging to the saturnine mysteries of time. Yet Chronos, as predicted by an oracle, was ousted by his son, Jupiter-Zeus, so that another class of gods, the twelve Olympians, could fulfill their role in the growth of the universe. We should note, however, that although Zeus became the new "Lord of the Universe," even he dared not violate the time laws imposed by his banished father. As the myths tell it, the gods of wisdom superseded the gods of time; once Time had been established, the twelvefold wisdom behind evolution could begin its work.

This twelvefold character of the universe is mirrored in the twelve bronze tablets of Roman Law, the twelve labors of Hercules, and the journey of Osiris through the twelve regions of the Underworld. Osiris led twelve apostles; Buddha enlightened twelve disciples; Ahura Mazda, the Persian sun god, directed twelve "Amshaspands"; Mahavira instructed twelve teachers; and St. Francis and his brothers numbered twelve. The legend of the Holy Grail tells us that Joseph of Arimathea was accompanied by twelve followers.

This repeated mention of the twelve as a scale of measurement reminds us that ancient weights and measures were originally taken from the proportions of the macrocosmic heavens and the microcosmic human body, and inscribed into the sacred geometry of temples, the practical methods of apportioning land, etc. Like the Pyramid of Giza and Solomon's Temple, the design of holy architecture was cosmically inspired.

The Rhythm of Wisdom

These snippets of mythology disclose something of the Jupiter-Zeus personality expressed in the relation of time and space and in the cosmic wisdom behind evolution as the ancients understood it. Thus, the twelve-year cycles of the planet Jupiter, "the King's Star," and the character of the Hellenistic Zeus have something in common: biography.

The significance of the twelve in biography and its kinship with the wisdom of Divine Law is perfectly illustrated by the twelve-year-old Jesus, "who tarried behind in Jerusalem," to discourse with the men of wisdom in the Temple. "They found him sitting in the midst of the doctors, both hearing them and asking them questions. And all that heard Him were astonished at His understanding and answers" (Luke 2:46-47). Frederick W. Farrar in his *Life of Christ* illustrates the high significance of the twelfth year in Jewish tradition. For example, Moses left the home of Pharaoh's daughter; Samuel's soul heard the voice of Jehovah; Solomon cast the first judgement which demonstrated his wisdom; and Josiah dreamed of his reforms. Farrar goes on to stress the social importance of this year in Jewish society. The twelve-year-old boy began to learn a trade according to the custom, and he was no longer available to be sold into slavery. At this time he was known as the "Son of the Law." In a nutshell, the psychological-spiritual changes taking place in every twelve-year-old is a miniature reflection of the immense spiritual adjustments occurring in the temple Jesus.

A brief comment or two on a handful of lives should ease our way into the major biography which comes later. The purpose of this exercise is to sense the link between the twelve-year rhythm and phases or bursts of creativity.

Any serious examination of a biographical time chart will disclose the presence of the twelve and its coordination with the rhythm of the seven. The illuminating idea that sacred architecture is frozen music helps us better visualize this mutuality. The seven, in a sense, is the melodic flow of purposeful time ordering the progressive advance of the psyche. The twelve on the other hand, imprints these themes on the destiny space of the physical world. The twelve, for example, fashions the architectural image of the soul's evolution in space, a superstructure built cycle by cycle, brick by brick. We should not assume that the biographical twelve is separate from the working of the seven.

Auspiciously, Isaac Newton (1642–1727) was born in the year Galileo died, twelve years after the death of Kepler. Born on Christmas Day, Newton always considered his destiny divinely inspired. His pursuit of truth was unquestionably motivated by his religious attitude toward science. First and foremost, his life and work was securely rooted in the belief that the universe was the handiwork of the supreme Father God. Despite his staunch religious convictions and mystical bent, however, this patriarch of science produced a sterile, mechanistic world-picture based on the absolute authority of observation and measurement. Although he also explored scripture, history, and even practical alchemy, his discoveries were solely confined to the cold corpse of the once-living universe. And naturally so, since what has been called the "Newtonian consciousness" is one-eyed and blind to the life hidden behind the veils of sense phenomena. His task was to weigh the body of the universe; it took a different kind of mind to intuit its soul and spirit. He stared at phenomena and deduced his famous laws using his forensic eye to examine the behavior of matter when acted upon by an external force. Yet for all his limitations, this Moses of the age of observation with his "spectator consciousness" (to borrow a term from Ernst Lehrs) still forms much of the foundation of modern science.

Between twenty-three and twenty-four, Newton experienced an extraordinary series of discoveries so momentous that scientific thought was revolutionized, and the rest of his long career was spent expounding upon and defending them. In a few brief months, Newton laid the basis for modern calculus and for the modern understanding of light and color. Most momentous of all, of course, was his theory of gravity. Newton described those few months in the plague years of 1665 and 1666, now known as the *annus mirabilis* (the wonderful year): "In those days I was in the prime of my age for invention, and minded Mathematics and Philosophy more than at any time since."

Like a mystic, he had directed the full force of his concentration onto a single point of observation. He dared, for instance, to stare directly at the indignant face of the sun and then examine its afterimage, its "phantasm." This, perhaps, was typical of his brilliant yet one-sided intellect and why he saw only the afterimages of life, only the shadow images of the Tao, the Cosmic Order he worshipped. Concerned only with the optical and mechanical behavior of light, he overlooked its aesthetic, psychological, and numinous qualities. His mind was the polar opposite of those such as Goethe's and Blake's. Yet during that brief but intense mind grind in 1666, his mathematical studies produced the basis of his calculus while the prismatic experiments led to his theory of colors. But the most striking feature of his "wonderful year" was his search for the universal laws of gravity. Without gravity, Newton's universe would have collapsed into a godless heap of chaos. His Lord was what

Nietzsche called "The Spirit of Gravity." Newton's earthbound senses weighed the carcass of the living universe. So when his famous apple fell from the "tree of Eden," he judged the manner of its fall and the pull of the earth, not the nature of the fruit or the mystery of its ascent!

Yet for all his limitations, Newton's brief surge of brilliance produced the underpinnings which remain today as the foundation of modern physics. The sensational discoveries in this brief period of his life are unequalled in the history of modern science. When Newton's Jupiter returned to its birth position, the twenty-four-year-old genius seized hold of the laws which would reign supreme in physics until amended by Einstein some two hundred and forty years later.

Newton and Albert Einstein (1879–1955), it seems, employed the same timekeeper. The same mysterious metronome triggered both of their bursts of discovery between twenty-three and twenty-five. Einstein was twenty-three (1902) when he joined the Swiss Patent Office. Working alone on the fringe of the scientific world, this obscure young mind probed, like his famous predecessor's, the mysteries of light and gravity. But Einstein took a mighty leap and found an elegant mathematical means to bring the two forms of energy together. At the same time, he dismantled Newton's old, rigid framework of absolute space and time and made them relative to the observer. The result was the Special Theory of Relativity (1905), which radically changed the whole character of physics and opened up tantalizing new vistas of the universe. Just as Newton pulled humanity away from the natural-magical flux of the ancients' universe, Einstein helped to get physics moving again toward the spiritual and mystical regions of reality. Of course, the realization that matter and energy are interchangeable was only the first step, but it gave physics a new lease on life. The thunderbolt of Jupiter-Zeus (the thunderbolt is an ancient symbol for idea and inspiration) that struck Newton, also electrified the mind of Albert Einstein at the same age—and ushered in the atomic age.

We have already touched on the life of Madame Curie (1867–1934) in the previous chapter, but of particular interest here are the three-year increments which together build up the twelve-year cycle. Marie completed her secondary studies at fifteen and at eighteen left her family and took a position as a governess to support her sister through the university. At twenty-one, she entered a laboratory in Warsaw, and her enrollment at the Sorbonne four days before her twenty-fourth birthday brought this cycle to a happy conclusion. Three years later she met her future husband, Pierre, and at thirty they launched the research that led to the isolation of radium. At thirty-three, the Curie's lamentable finances forced Marie to sacrifice some of her precious time to teach. But this cycle reached a glorious conclusion when Marie was thirty-six and she and Pierre shared the Nobel Prize with Becquerel. During the following cycle, between thirty-six and forty-eight, despite Pierre's tragic death when she was thirty-eight, she set herself the task of consolidating their work on radioactivity and stimulating the interest of the medical world. At forty-five, she received the Nobel Prize for physics and also founded the Institute of Radium in Paris, which was completed when she was forty-eight, a year which coincided with the outbreak of World War I. The war dramatized the urgent need for radiography to examine the injured soldiers. This meant that Madame Curie had to train technicians and adapt vehicles to carry the equipment to field hospitals. During her next twelve-year cycle, between forty-eight and sixty, Madame Curie's work reached the global stage, when she was invited to serve the League of Nations. Thus, cycle after cycle, from the years of preparation to her involvement with radium and its technical and therapeutical applications, her twelve-year cycles shaped the pattern of her career.

Although, by and large, the twelve-year rhythm appears to govern spells of creativity and the development of ideas, it can also be found in the relationship between couples. It is, therefore, especially relevant to marriages. We can see this in the life of Eleanor Roosevelt (1884–1962) whose destiny was closely synchronized with that of her husband. After a serious operation in her twenty-fourth year, Eleanor struggled to adjust herself to marriage and child-raising while supporting Franklin's blossoming career. Obviously, it was not a creative span in the scientific sense, but to her the task seemed as daunting as Marie Curie's search for radium. Eleanor was thirty-six when her husband was stricken with polio, just as his political star seemed to be approaching its zenith. Eleanor's whole cycle between thirty-six and forty-eight was completely devoted to his courageous climb back into the national limelight. After nursing him through the critical stages of his illness and encouraging his physical and mental adjustment to paralysis, she was forty-eight when she shared the triumph of his election to the presidency. The span between forty-eight and sixty was an exciting and expansive one for her. Besides fulfilling her private and public duties, she wrote articles, books, and radio scripts. But the end of this period brought another radical change. World War II and the strain of command completely undermined Franklin's delicate health, and he died when she was sixty. After twelve years in the White House, Eleanor faced another immense transition. In her *Autobiography* she relates how she rode down the old White House elevator in that April of 1945 with a mood of sadness and anxiety, "because I was saying good-bye to an unforgettable era and I had given little thought to the fact that from this day forward I would be on my own." But this new cycle opened another door of opportunity when she was invited to work for the newly born United Nations. She devoted seven years to its troublesome childhood before retiring. At seventy-two, she returned to politics to campaign for Adlai Stevenson in his second unsuccessful bid for the presidency. Her closing years were both creative and influential, partly because Franklin Roosevelt had been so venerated at home and abroad, and most assuredly because of her social work, her compassionate and energetic concern for the global family of humanity.

LEO TOLSTOY—MAN OF CONSCIENCE

The destiny of Leo Tolstoy (1828–1910) and the creative dynamic force behind his quest to fathom the nature of good and evil remorselessly engineered his spiritual growth and his prodigious attempts to bring a moral form to every facet of his daily life. It is not the brilliance of his literary genius that often comforts me in my dark moments, but rather the manner of his tortuous journey to uncover the meaning of his life. He is, indeed, the brother of every seeking soul.

There was an astonishing rapport between his genius and his motherland. Tolstoy, like Dostoyevsky and many Russian artists, was nourished by the mind of the Russian folk-soul. Such men were the guides, the teachers, and the conscience of the people. Their books were read to or by everyone from the rough peasant to the aristocracy. Tolstoy's conscience was undoubtedly a vital part of the Russian psyche. Despite all his inconsistencies and limitations, he fought to fit everything into his own moral-logical scheme of things.

Tolstoy's enormous literary dimensions could never conceal the fact that he was such a human fellow. In fact, it is his stubbornness, arrogance, and wild contradictions that make him so approachable. He was much loved for his fearless defense of the oppressed against the political, religious, and legal establishments. His innate sense of wonder, compassion, and conscience was effervescent; these three elements were responsible for his artistic relationship to nature and the human condition. No wonder children adored him.

Tolstoy's seven-year span between forty-two and forty-nine was a protracted and painful spiritual crisis. He traced his passage through his Dark Wood in one of the most instructive books ever written, *A Confession*. This cycle, which brought about the emergence and clarity of his morality, completely reshaped his life on every level.

In a nutshell, then, Tolstoy's inner journey led him from his battle for self-mastery to the awakening of a practical living faith. As an artist he was able to express his personal evolution in his novels, which are the beacons marking the stages of his ascent. The novel has a form shaped by passing time; its movement allows us to accompany the characters on a journey through time and events. The novel, therefore, has a psychological closeness, since the writer unfolds his characters, often aspects of himself, creating and dealing with experience in time. Thus the novel is a form of biography. Tolstoy's novels permit us to assess the progress of his inner development at different stages of his journey. Woven into their dramatic content are the themes which concerned him all his life: the serf question, government, religion, and social attitudes. But one of the central motifs, growing in emphasis with each novel, is the *relationship between man and woman*.

Each novel occupied a crucial position along his unfolding path of inner growth, and this is what we will trace through his twelve-year cycles. But we cannot unravel the significance of the man-woman theme without first looking deeper into his complex psyche. Tolstoy's soul was both tutored and tortured by his formidable conscience, a voice which, like Dostoevsky, mercilessly compelled him to scrutinize the working of good and evil in himself. He was ever suspended in the web of his dilemmas, teetering on the edge between his natural passions and his higher aspirations, between his convictions and the entrenched mores of the Russian establishment. Indeed, his conscience was his absolute authority, one needing no validation. His courageous yet stumbling efforts to obey it reaped an inevitable harvest of scorn, especially when he tried to adjust his way of life to his emerging beliefs. Thus, Tolstoy was a man in conflict with himself until forty-eight or forty-nine, and thereafter in conflict with the social attitudes of Russia, and even with his own family. At the very core of this inner tension stood the conflict between the masculine and feminine elements in his own psyche. Tolstoy experienced conflict, first in his personal relationship with women, second in the antagonism between his new religious faith and the masculine symbols of dogma and power exemplified by the Church and State.

On a lower, more instinctive and immediate level, he struggled with his own carnality. The struggle between flesh and spirit was a primal conflict in this sensual and passionate Russian who loved women with a violent intensity. For most of his life he was thrown hither and thither in this vortex fighting for control and vigorously condemning this side of himself and its presence in others. He viewed the erotic as an evil masked by the entrancing veils of poetry and virtue. All this, however, served as fuel for his conscience.

On a higher level, Tolstoy's moral confusion is symptomatic of the drift of a modern consciousness which attempts to defeat the old tyranny of sexuality now that the once clearly defined roles of the sexes are dissolving. Besides its moral and social overtones, this conflict between masculine and feminine, given prominent attention by Jung, is a reflection of the psychological discord in the psyche of every modern man and woman. Thus, hidden within the man-woman problem is a deeper question: What is the real nature of the individual psyche? This is one reason Tolstoy's novels have retained their wide appeal. Although Freud, Adler, and especially Jung, lifted this enigma into a clearer light, Tolstoy transformed it into the consummate artistry of his novels.

As Tolstoy's consciousness matured, this theme was elevated and refined, novel by novel, through the workings of his twelve-year rhythm.

We will use the following list of Tolstoy's works with his age when he wrote them to show the development of the man-woman theme as he progressed through the cycles:

Childhood:	23-24
Family Happiness:	30-year transition
War and Peace:	35-41
Anna Karenina:	44-48
The Kreutzer Sonata:	60-61 1/2
Resurrection:	60-71 1/2

Of course, it is difficult to locate in time the expansion of ideas stirring the genesis of each novel. Research indicates, however, that a major impetus or completion occurred when Tolstoy's Jupiter passed through its natal zodiacal sign.

BIRTH TO TWELVE: The lustre of Tolstoy's early years is beautifully reflected in *Childhood*. He loved and cherished these memories, which continued to warm and delight his soul throughout his lifetime. He saw the innocent joy and unbounded need to love as the major motives present in his formative years. There was plenty of rich nourishment for the heart and mind of young Tolstoy on the family estate at Yasnaya Polyana, with its farms and peasants, its bustling household and summer visitors. There were carefree summers among streams, meadows, stables, and woods, and contented winters in the midst of the white wilderness, safe in the rambling house which was a sanctum of family warmth and order. He was an active and warmhearted child, fascinated by the variety of resident and visiting characters at Yasnaya Polyana, including the little girls who so easily captivated him! Indeed, his childhood was a treasure chest which he drew upon throughout his adult life. Much of it would be resurrected in his novels and stories with no loss of freshness, detail or charm. He deeply appreciated the value of the domestic influence that shaped his outlook. His Aunt Tatiana, for one, had a profound influence on his life. In his *Reminiscences* he valued her gift of the spiritual joy of loving. He sensed her happiness in loving, her appreciation of a quiet life, her pleasant relationships with other people, and her absence of hurry.

Another impression which fertilized his imagination was a story-game invented by his brother Nicholas. This was no trivial game, however, since it demonstrates the elemental power story-symbols can generate in a young soul; it was a stimulus which never ceased to work in the deeper levels of his psyche. In his *Reminiscences,* Tolstoy records that when he was five his brother Nicholas announced that he had a secret which, when disclosed, would dissolve all trouble, anger, and disease. It would enable everyone to love one another. Nicholas said that he had inscribed this secret on a green stick which he had buried at the edge of a ravine. Tolstoy later asked to be buried at this place. When over seventy, he spoke again of this magic stick: he said that as he once believed in its message, so he now believed that such a truth really exists, and that it would be revealed and then fulfill all its promises.

Four times the happiness of that enfabled homestead was eclipsed by the gloom of black drapery, whispered burial preparations, and grief. He lost his mother at two, his father at nine, his grandmother at ten, and his aunt at twelve. Not unnaturally, these events made him acutely aware of the impermanence of life. To counter his fear of the unknown, he took serious steps to implement one of his new ideas. He suddenly remembered that death had its eye on him at every moment. He decided, therefore, ("surprised that men had not understood it before me") that happiness lay only in the present moment. For three days, he neglected his lessons by lying in bed reading novels and eating spice cakes!

He felt everything intensely and was nicknamed "Lyova Royova" (Leo Crybaby), and sharp words or even praise could turn on his tears. Even when he was a child, a bout of exuberance would be followed by grave introspection, and he was beset by remorse whenever he brought displeasure to anyone. He later remembered that he was continuously preoccupied with himself: he was always conscious, rightly or wrongly, of what people thought of him, and he worried about the feelings he inspired in those around him.

Troyat's memorable biography, *Tolstoy*, mentions the early signs of Tolstoy's awakening conscience. He states that the young Tolstoy looked into his own soul for the answers to the mysteries that surrounded him. His tutor, who felt that he was a lazy good-for-nothing, was amazed by his intellectual precocity. Formal study bored him stiff, but "he explored his own conscience with a degree of insight that was uncanny in a boy of twelve." Leo devised rules of conduct for himself which were beyond his willpower, but it was the exercise of his conscience that mattered. Tolstoy's tutors despaired of rousing his interest in formal lessons, although one of them considered him to be a "young Molière." At twelve, however, he was already testing his pen by writing a highly patriotic version of the Napoleonic wars. This gives us our first hint of the connection between his literary path and the twelve-year cycles.

TWELVE TO TWENTY-FOUR: Soon after crossing the threshold of adolescence, Tolstoy tasted the bittersweet fruit of independence by courting the mistress of ideas and pitting his conscience against his burgeoning physical appetites. His university career floundered on boredom since his *daimon* abhorred the cold mental discipline needed for the study of law. A fever that sent him to the hospital when he was eighteen was nothing serious, but it marks a turning point halfway through this cycle. At that time he wrote that he should be the unhappiest man alive if he did not have a purpose in life, and that he invariably arrived at the conclusions that the purpose of our human existence is to afford a maximum of help toward the most complete development of everything that exists.

Using his sickness as an excuse to leave the university, he returned to Yasnaya Polyana to manage the four thousand acres and three hundred serfs he had inherited. But despite his interest in their welfare and education, he soon tired of the routine and began chasing the glamorous distractions of city life. The young count succumbed to feverish rounds of gambling and womanizing which always ended in debt, guilt, and sessions of self-purging. Women, be they society belles or gypsy girls, intrigued and tormented him. Rationalizing his moral dilemma, he set himself the rule to "regard the company of women as a necessary evil and avoid them as much as possible. Who indeed is the cause of sensuality, indolence and frivolity and all sorts of vice in us if not women?" These spasms of degrading behavior brought him some excitement and much self-contempt, but his battle with his conscience deepened his contact with his awakening psyche.

We should also note in this cycle two particularly significant influences which helped to shape his thinking and goals. One offered him a picture of what the human being appears to be, the other an image of what the human being can become. He claimed that Rousseau and the Gospel of St. Matthew had set him on the road to the good. He read all Rousseau's twenty volumes, recognizing all too clearly in himself the author's disconcerting list of vices and flaws resident in human nature. On the other hand, the Sermon on the Mount ("Lift not thy hand against evil") offered him a pertinent morality, a rock on which he could build a personal religion. The idea of not resisting evil became a powerful force in his life and work. Later, this message would be passed on to Gandhi and the Indian methods of civil disobedience, eventually finding its way into the heart of Martin Luther King and the American civil rights movement.

Near the end of this cycle, Tolstoy accompanied his brother Nicholas to the Caucasus, where they experienced army life and warfare for the first time. Leo was both repelled and stimulated by the general debauchery and superficiality of the officers. Despite this bog of temptation, he managed to work on his first novel. Completed when he was twenty-four, *Childhood* is a mixture of his early life at Yasnaya Polyana and the life of a Muscovite family. It is a translucent picture of family life with all its humor and pathos seen through the eyes of a child. Representing the first rung of his literary ladder, *Childhood*, with its refreshing candor, was acclaimed by the critics.

TWENTY-FOUR TO THIRTY-SIX: Tolstoy's diary records that on his twenty-fourth birthday he felt that he had achieved absolutely nothing in his life. He suspected that there was a meaning to his struggle with doubt and passion, but he could not really sense the direction of his destiny.

As a commissioned officer, present at the bloody siege of Sevastopol, he observed the hideous destruction of minds and bodies and shared the comradeship and heroism of men under fire. It was this direct experience of battle which later inspired the striking realism of *War and Peace*. His vivid essay on the battle of Sevastopol so impressed the Czar that he offered to have the young man removed from danger. About that same time, Tolstoy was almost killed by a grenade.

Unable to resist the gambling and womanizing escapades of his fellow officers, his conscience gave him no end of trouble. With all his soul he wished to be good, and when he was completely alone he sought goodness. When he tried to express his most sincere desire, namely to be morally good, he felt that he met only contempt and ridicule; but as soon as he yielded to nasty passions, he was then praised and encouraged! He nevertheless continued his rhythm of reckless behavior followed by self-analysis and exorcism of his various evils. Time and again his diary records this self-inquisition. He kept insisting to himself that the most important thing in his life was his efforts to correct the vices of laziness, lack of character, and bad temper.

Tolstoy returned to Yasnaya Polyana to reorganize the estate, develop his writing, and reopen his little school. He championed the cause of the serfs by writing *Landlord's Warning*. By being born into the aristocracy he was a landowner with almost absolute power over his serfs. His conscience, however, grew uneasy over the inequality of human rights and later urged him to repudiate his privilege by adopting the simple ways of the *muzhik* (peasant). By then he was in the throes of the major psychological change between twenty-eight and thirty. His formative cycle was nearly over, but it had given him a wealth of experience: a rich family life, an interest in education and social reform, army life, a belief in the need for a non-dogmatic faith, and his first literary success. Nonetheless, he was still uncertain of his future, and he was as critical as ever of his lack of inner progress. In a letter to Alexandria Tolstoy in 1858, he wrote that when he looked at himself, he saw only a daydreaming egotist, one incapable of becoming anything else. He lamented the fact that when one concentrates on love of self and self-indulgence, it is difficult to activate one's love of others and self-denial.

As we might expect, *Family Happiness*, the novel written at the thirtieth-year transition was a fundamental one dealing with the disharmony between the sexes. The theme was still rudimentary, but he allowed husband and wife to settle down to a life of domestic contentment once they had emancipated themselves from the passions and aggressiveness impeding the development of their union. Tolstoy's own marriage at thirty-four to his eighteen-year-old bride, Sonya, provided the creative and temptation-free space he needed for the sustained burst of energy which brought forth *War and Peace*.

War and Peace (which was planned in his thirtieth year) is a national epic, a spectacle of gigantic proportions covering every dimension of human life. It has everything: aristocrats and serfs, officers and privates, courtiers and diplomats, country life and town life. There are flirtations, love affairs, balls, hunts, social reforms, and the customs of battlefield, boudoir, and drawing room. Beneath this welter of social phenomena, however, Tolstoy explores the nature of power. He wonders whether history is constructed by the individual's self-will or by the unconscious, corporate will of the people—the will of the "folk-soul." He depicts war as the catalyst of change. When individuals, families, and nations collide with the dissolving forces of chaos, they are brutally awakened; conflict engenders consciousness. The exterior of this vast social tableau, however, is fashioned around the family, and within the family we find the nucleus, the man-woman conflict. There we find Andrey being betrayed by Natasha's affair with Pierre. Tolstoy shows us souls besieged by passion, avarice, guilt, and desire in a story bristling with characters and events. He also depicts how the many-leveled workings of good and evil are exposed when war tears down the facades which people construct to hide their true natures. Sounding throughout all this is the irrepressible voice of Tolstoy's conscience.

THIRTY-SIX TO FORTY-EIGHT: Sonya's loving care and reliable business sense protected Tolstoy from outside pressures and temptations. By day, she managed the estate, fussed over the children, and kept the domestic rhythm in order, while at night she deciphered her husband's innumerable alterations and copied out the new pages of *War and Peace*. But the happiness they shared was not to last. After the completion of his great novel, Tolstoy slipped into crisis, his entrance to the Dark Wood. The beginning of his desperate search for faith was heralded by an unnerving vision of his own death in the town of Arzamus, in August 1869; he was forty-one years old. After a restless night of sinister dreamlike visions, his unease turned to panic.

He recorded this intense incident in an unfinished story which he called, "Notes of a Madman." He told himself his depression was ridiculous. To the query as to the source of his depression came the answer "the presence of death." Realizing that death was present, a cold shudder ran through him. Though it had nothing to do with him at that moment, he sensed its inevitable threat. He felt death at work, and for Tolstoy, this was a terrifying experience. Seeking to shake it off, he looked about him at the real world. Even the stump of his candle told the same story. There is nothing in life, nothing exists except death, and he railed against this injustice. Death should not be! This is a particularly trenchant example of psychological change, the disturbance associated with the seven-year cycle between forty-two and forty-nine.

Sonya, of course, was worried by her husband's disorientation. "He engaged in long laborious meditations, often he said his brain hurt him, some painful process was going on inside it, everything was over for him, it was time for him to die." Regardless of all his home comforts and literary success, Tolstoy suddenly found himself on the precarious edge of meaninglessness with no sense of direction. He seemed to be standing in his own light; no matter how hard he tried, he could see nothing but the senselessness of his personal existence. What Tolstoy feared most, however, was not death itself but the loss of his soul, the terrifying loss of self. From our vantage point, we can see there is nothing unnatural in his predicament, since it represents the sloughing off of one psychological skin to uncover a deeper level of identity and self-meaning.

Anna Karenina, Tolstoy's third great novel, was written during the second half of his crisis, begun at forty-four and completed when he was forty-nine. There we find that the man-woman theme has matured since *War and Peace*. The battalions of characters and incidents in *War and Peace* faded from view; this time, he plumbed the depths of two families with all his insight and descriptive skill. His twelve-year cycle had transformed the archetypal triangle of Pierre, Natasha, and Andrey into Vronsky, Anna, and Karenin. This is a story of marriage and separation in which Tolstoy concentrates on the triangle of lover, wife, and husband. He examines the effects of adultery, the results of possessiveness and guilt, and the intolerable social pressures brought to bear on poor Anna. Exploring his characters as he explored himself, with a ruthless psychological scalpel, he makes Anna's ordeal touch our feelings—and our conscience.

Actually, the character of Anna went through quite a metamorphosis during the book's development. Early versions depict her as an unscrupulous, vindictive, and unsavory example of womanhood. As the novel matured, the men who fought over her soul and body degenerated into narrow, one-sided creatures. Vronsky became a blustering officer goaded by passion, while Karenin turned into an elderly bureaucrat driven by ambition. Anna's soul is swept into a vortex of irreconcilable forces, her longing for love, her sense of duty, the cruel demands of her men, and the intolerance of public opinion. There is no doubt that her suicide aggravated the conscience of Russian society. The gossip, praise, and argument it provoked clearly shows that Tolstoy had touched a raw nerve in countless individuals.

FORTY-EIGHT TO SIXTY: Tolstoy's inner transformation between forty-two and forty-nine radically altered his writing and his way of life. After years of doubt and distress, he uncovered a faith which could sustain him. At last he had emerged from his Dark Wood. How then had he found his way to the personal meaning of his life? He had pondered the answers of the rational and the metaphysical thinkers but found that they, for all their wisdom, were confounded by the mystery of death. In his *Confession*, he described his position as being "terrible." He could uncover nothing along the path of reasonable knowledge except a denial of life. Of course, there was always faith, but faith for him meant the denial of reason. He felt that to uncover the meaning of existence he had to destroy all reason, yet reason is why meaning is desired in the first place! It was a ridiculous dilemma.

No matter how diligently he rummaged in the attics of philosophy and theology, he could not find his solutions there. But the mists began to clear when he looked into the heart of the simple *muzhik*. He learned to love these people. In his *Confession* he said that the more he knew about their lives, the more he loved them and the easier it became for him to live. These ordinary folk, the very backbone of humankind, stood firm under the blows of famine, pestilence, and war, upheld by their implacable faith in God and a life which would outlast death. Tolstoy realized that faith is the strength of life, the true source. One had to believe in something—in the infinite. Without faith, one could not live. He now understood his error. He understood that to his question of what his life was, his answer—an evil—was quite correct. The only mistake was that the answer referred only to *his* life, while he had referred it to life in general. Really, his life, a life of indulgence and desires, was senseless and evil, and therefore the reply that life was evil and an absurdity referred only to his own life, not to the life of humankind.

Tolstoy described this struggle as his search for God. He said that the search for God is not a process of reason, but a feeling. It proceeded from the heart, not his thinking, which stood as a barrier to the life-sustaining energies of faith. This was no Pascalian flash of revelation but a slow and painful dawning. Born anew, Tolstoy then offered Russia the harvest of his agony in a stream of moral essays and parables which examined the working of love and evil in society. Standing on the battlements of his convictions, he dared to accuse the Church of intellectual dishonesty. This dishonesty, he declared, is why Christianity is incapable of bridging the gap between abstruse theology and the living truth of the Gospels which shows us how to live. Bowing to nothing save conscience, Tolstoy struggled to uncover the meaning of the Gospels. His *Confession*, begun in 1879, records the steps of his awakening. This emergence triggered a burst of moral essays; he wrote *The Critique of Dogmatic Theology* in 1880 and *The Union of the Gospels* (based on the Sermon on the Mount) in 1882. *What I Believe* formulated his thoughts on nonresistance to evil, while *What Then Must We Do?* was inspired by a visit to the Moscow slums.

As Tolstoy drew closer to the people, his everyday life underwent a dramatic change. This nobleman, for example, began stitching his own boots, chopping wood, and helping his peasants build and harvest. He would be dependent on no one. In a letter to Rolland Romain, he wrote about his moment of truth in which he found that in our depraved society—the society of so-called civilized people—manual labor was essential, solely because the chief defect of that society had been and still was that people make every effort to avoid working themselves, and exploit the labor of the poor, ignorant, and unhappy classes who are their slaves, giving them nothing in return. He realized that he could never again believe in the sincerity of the Christian who sent his servant to empty his chamber pot. The simplest ethical precept was to be served by others as little as possible and to serve others as much as possible.

One moment his family saw him buried in the study of Hebrew or theology, the next, striding about dressed as a *muzhik*. But as Tolstoy found his moral path, so his conflict with his family increased. He urged them to simplify their lives and suggested that they strengthen their spirits by manual labor. But Sonya could not keep up with him, and the rift between them widened.

Another great novel was born at age sixty, when the twelve-year and thirty-year cycles reached their conjunction. *The Kreutzer Sonata*, begun in June 1889, is a higher octave of

Anna Karenina and *Family Happiness*. The latter, written thirty years earlier, observed marriage through the eyes of a woman who had transferred her love for her husband to her children. *Family Happiness* presents Tolstoy's ideas in larval form, and *The Kreutzer Sonata* shows us how they had matured during the Saturn cycle.

The major character, Pozdeshev, tells his fellow passengers on a train how he murdered his wife out of jealousy. This novel bears the imprint of Tolstoy's own disintegrating marriage. He injected all the venom of his resentment into his description of the decay of the Pozdeshev family. Gone is the felicity of *War and Peace*; the Pozdeshev marriage is stifled by sensuality and jealousy. Regardless of all the years of Sonya's sacrifice and support, Tolstoy unmercifully exposed their most intimate secrets.

Sonya also kept a diary. She knew that everyone felt sorry for her, from the emperor down. But she did not need to consult the opinions of others to realize that. Deep down in her own heart, she always felt that the book was directed against her. It mutilated and humiliated her in the eyes of the whole world, and destroyed everything they had preserved of love for one another.

Besides revealing Tolstoy's frustration, *The Kreutzer Sonata* also reflects his view of marriage, based on the passage: "Everyone that looketh on woman to lust after her hath committed adultery with her already in his own heart" (Matthew 5:28). In his afterword, Tolstoy declared that the Christian ideal is the love of God and one's fellow man. Sexual love and marriage, on the other hand, he viewed as a service of self and therefore an obstacle to these spiritual ideals. In other words, the lower ingredients of marriage tend to impede the development of a real psychological relationship between husband and wife.

Tolstoy's conscience had won many victories, but now he tackled his oldest and most persistent passion: sex. *The Kreutzer*

Sonata magnifies the destructive effect of lust *inside* marriage, which narrows the husband's acknowledgment and benefit of womanhood and pushes the relationship toward alienation and breakdown. In other words, desire, jealousy, and possessiveness obliterate the husband's realization of his wife's individuality and right to self-fulfillment. Tolstoy's judgement was extreme, and he courageously overstated his view. Despite the fact that this novel prescribed complete chastity between husband and wife, his own wife gave birth at about that same time to their thirteenth child! But to judge Tolstoy, as flawed as any man, on his contradictions, completely misses the point of his destiny and its lasting achievements. For Tolstoy, chastity was an ideal, something one should strive for, although virtually unattainable. He believed that husband and wife could fashion a union based on the union of selves rather than of bodies. Naturally, he was mocked and misunderstood: *The Kreutzer Sonata*, which had to be printed underground, brought forth a storm of abuse and attacks from the pulpit.

SIXTY TO SEVENTY-TWO: Although Tolstoy went to great lengths to narrow the gap between what he preached and what he practiced, his attempts were attacked with growing intensity. In a letter of 1892, he assented that his controversial contradictions stemmed from weakness, not errors in moral judgement. He protested that he was not a saint and had never proclaimed himself as one. He was a man, often carried away, and sometimes, or rather always, unable to say exactly what he thought and felt—not that he did not want to say it, but that he often exaggerated or simply blundered. In his deeds the case was yet worse, for he was only a weak man of vicious habits who wished to serve the God of truth but who constantly went astray. As he saw it, when people considered him one who cannot make a mistake, every error seemed like a lie. But if he were understood to be a weak man, the discord could rather be seen as a sign of weakness. Then he would appear to be what he was, a sorry but sincere man striving to be a worthy servant of God.

But the more he was vilified by the Establishment, the more the pilgrims flocked to Yasnaya Polyana to observe or be counseled. Tolstoy had become an international sage and the moral beacon of Russia. Motley groups known as the "Tolstoyans" had begun to practice the "new morality," while other revolutionaries welcomed his reforms but dismissed his Christianity. He had become a conspicuous force in Russia's awakening. Indeed, he responded to the looming age of revolution long before Marx or Lenin did.

Tolstoy was far from being a political creature. But this arch critic of society excavated and sifted the choking dust of centuries of tradition and dogma, searching for a living morality which could heal the wretchedness of the times. He spoke out against the stultifying influence of church and state, condemning prejudice and falsehood wherever it lurked. In civic circles, he was regarded as an extremist. He extolled a classless society founded on a moral order of conscience and compassion, not the soul-diminishing tyranny which later took its slogans from Marx. Thus, Tolstoy was no grim prophet of communism; he knew that only a truly moral order could create a healthy social order. His was the way of love and spiritual discipline. He saw property and institutions as paralytic evils impeding the growth of community. The society he sought would grow from the individual's search for the energy, cohesion, and selflessness of Christian morality. Because Tolstoy was regarded as a dangerous anarchist, the state took steps to silence him. His women rallied to the rescue. His aunt, Countess Tolstoy, begged the emperor not to act on the charges which would put her nephew in prison, and Sonya persuaded the Czar to lift the ban on *The Kreutzer Sonata*, the novel which had so humiliated her.

Despite Sonya's magnanimity, however, their marriage was further undermined by Chertkov, Tolstoy's chief disciple. While

Sonya accused him of turning her husband against her, the Tolstoyans blamed her for preventing Tolstoy from practicing his principles. For a while, however, the tension eased as the great famine of 1891-92 drew the family together. With common purpose, they set about alleviating the starvation all around them. Tolstoy wrote articles and helped his children distribute supplies, while Sonya kept the accounts and appealed for money from Europe and grain from America. There were moments of tenderness and even passion, but the wounds would not heal. Sonya's diary (1892) records her frustration. After one of their numerous quarrels, Leo had reaffirmed his passionate love and commitment. But she felt it was all physical. Despite the passion she also shared, she had always dreamed of a platonic connection, "a perfect spiritual communion." Sonya was also greatly irritated by her husband's new lifestyle. In her diary (1885) she expressed her complaints. Leo's insistence on a vegetarian diet meant that two menus had to be prepared. His sermons on universal love resulted in a loss of feeling for his own family; his private life was now open to anyone and everyone; and his renunciation of earthly goods led him to criticize others.

At the same time, Tolstoy's own diary reveals his frustrations. He felt oppressed and sick at heart. He could not restrain himself in his desire to perform some great deed, and he wanted to devote the rest of his life to God, but felt that God either did not want him or did not want to encourage him in the direction he had chosen. It made him irritable to see the luxury created from the commerce in his books. He wanted to suffer, to trumpet forth this truth that was consuming him. His annoyance, however, did not slow his pen. *Christ and Patriotism* enraged both politicians and churchmen by suggesting that Christianity destroys patriotism and the worship of the state. *The Kingdom of God Is within You* condemned the repressive force used by government to perpetuate the feudalism which protects the wealthy. During the period he also wrote *What is*

Art?, *The Meaning of the Russian Revolution*, and *The Slavery of Our Times*.

Tolstoy's books were stations along his life's way. The last major novel, written between his sixtieth and seventy-second year, completed the series on the man-woman theme. Time and its rhythms had helped him digest his experiences, refine his morality, and exalt his consciousness. He was finally equipped to deliver his crowning expression. Before we look at the culmination of the twelve-year cycles in the *Resurrection*, let us glance back at the sequence of his writings so far. In *Childhood*, written at twenty-four, two families are seen through the eyes of a child, whereas the two families in *War and Peace* (thirty-six) are set against a background of war. In *Anna Karenina* (forty-eight), the social universe of *War and Peace* contracts into a sharply focused analysis of two families, while *The Kreutzer Sonata* (sixty) examines a single family ravaged by jealousy.

In *Resurrection*, the man-woman theme reaches its culmination. In fact, the woman dissolves altogether, leaving us with the hero and his tortuous self-transformation, his spiritual rebirth— his resurrection. This novel was born when a prosecutor told Tolstoy about a young nobleman who had been called to sit on a jury to judge a prostitute accused of theft. To the nobleman's consternation, however, he recognized the pitiful creature in the dock as the woman he had seduced and abandoned years before. In fact, his selfish desires had contributed to her downfall. Stricken with guilt, he vowed to make amends by marrying her, but she died before he could fulfill his promise. In the novel, the anguish of Nekhlydov's conscience is the coercive force which transmutes his attitude to himself and to life by awakening his moral sense. Thus the skein of good and evil, selflessness and egoism, freedom and bondage, passing through Tolstoy's earlier novels is finally disentangled when conscience achieves the birth of the "new man." Tolstoy came to believe that to describe the phenomenon of inner transformation and rebirth is one of the greatest but most difficult tasks of art.

Tolstoy's novels, under the progression of the twelve-year cycle, show the slow clarification of the man-woman theme. Seen from a modern psychological viewpoint, Tolstoy illustrates the excessiveness of the one-sided male who is chained to his lower instincts or trapped by logic. Such a man is uncreative, unimaginative, and powerless to communicate his deepest feelings. Deaf to conscience, ignorant of the subtlety of the heart, he passes straight from thought to action or is merely reactive. He who rejects the feminine in himself rejects his creator, his muse, his "imaginator," and thereby destroys his power to think creatively. The one-sided male, weak in conscience, on the one hand blocks the development of women, while, on the other, he is a danger to the world if ever he achieves power. History is riddled with such vultures who feed on the weak and unwary. Tolstoy's novels shed light on the riddle of the sexes and the tension in every person between masculine and feminine, which is nothing less than the source of our self-awareness, the struggle of the innermost self to command both soul and body.

The fading away of the woman in *Resurrection* highlights the emergence of the newborn ego. Thus, the woman, representing the feminine nature of the psyche, has been transformed by the conflict between the psyche's spiritual, emotional, and sensual components. The feminine has not been rejected or annihilated. It has been transformed into a love-filled morality—*eros* is transmuted into *amor* and then into *agape*. Tolstoy shows us that the relationship between man and woman and between the male and female sides of the psyche leads to higher union and liberation, a spiritual marriage. But more, when the ego is no longer enslaved by lower desires, it turns outward into the world to recreate society. This higher union of marriage, he says, will itself interpenetrate and regenerate the social environment. Tolstoy points out that the one-sided male, who exploits the female for his own gratification, not only destroys her but also destroys his own capacity for self-fulfillment. In a nutshell, Tolstoy believed that the man-woman conflict is the catalyst, conscience is the energy, and Christianity is the moral purpose to personal rebirth and social reform.

SEVENTY-TWO TO DEATH: The old man tried his utmost to secure the peace and simple poverty he yearned for to prepare for death, but conflict had forged his destiny and would not release him yet. He had become a force to be reckoned with in Russia, and he felt it his duty to speak out against the state's violent response to the growing discontent. The director of the *New Times* noted, "We have two Czars, Nicholas II and Leo Tolstoy. Which is the stronger? Nicholas is powerless against Tolstoy and cannot make him tremble on his throne. Whereas Tolstoy is incontestably shaking the throne of Nicholas II and his whole dynasty."

The Orthodox Church, unable to stem his growing influence, excommunicated him when he was seventy-two. The Synod's edict stated that God had permitted a new false prophet to appear in their midst. Led astray by pride, he had boldly and insolently dared to oppose God. Openly and in sight of all, he had denied the mother who had nurtured him and brought him up, the Orthodox Church; and he had devoted his literary talent to spreading doctrines which were contrary to Christ and the church, and to undermining the people's faith in their Father. The church, therefore, no longer counted him among her children and could not do so until he had repented and restored himself to communion with her. Tolstoy's reply drew attention to the need to return to first principles. He said that he believed in God, whom he conceived as the Spirit, Love, and Principle of all things. He believed God was in him as he was in God. He believed that the will of God was never more clearly expressed than in the doctrine of the Christ-Man. He believed that the purpose of our individual lives was to augment the sum of love for God and that this added measure of love would secure daily increasing happiness for us in this life, and in the life to come. He believed that there was only one means of progressing in love: prayer. Not public prayer in temples, which was condemned, he said, by Christ (Matthew 6:5-13), but solitary prayer, as He Himself had taught us, which consists in restoring and strengthening within oneself an awareness of the meaning of life and a belief that we must be ruled by the will of God.

There were processions and noisy demonstrations as the people rose to his defense, and the petulant old rebel had more influence than ever. The faithful descended on Yasnaya Polyana in droves to pay homage, but Tolstoy himself was displeased by all the fuss and waste. His diary reflected his emotions. He noted an aching pain caused by a sense of the shameful life he had lived surrounded by people who worked and slaved and only just managed to avoid dying of cold and hunger. All his visitors gorged themselves on spice cakes while others broke their necks getting all that "swill" ready for the table. He saw everybody working except himself. He felt an increasing need to describe all the folly and ignominy of those lives of luxury and brutality surrounded by starving, half-naked people, whom he described as being eaten alive by vermin, living in chicken coops.

His alienation from his family became even more obvious when he became trapped in the crossfire between Chertkov and a highly emotional Sonya, who was in the throes of a nervous breakdown. This friction, exacerbated by disputes over his will, diaries, and copyrights, made his life absolutely unbearable. He had tried to leave home before, but now he was determined to try again to find a haven somewhere. In a farewell letter to Sonya, he wrote that he was aware that his departure would cause her pain, and he was sorry about that; but she should try to understand him and believe that he could not do otherwise. He felt that his position in the house was becoming intolerable. The luxury which had always surrounded him was becoming impossible to bear, and he felt the time had come for him to give up the world, and spend his last days alone and in silence. He begged her to understand this and not come rushing after him.

The eighty-two-year-old refugee slipped away from home, only to be taken ill on the journey. Instead of a sanctuary of peace, he found himself in a stationmaster's bed in the tiny country station of Astapovo, besieged by hordes of government officials, doctors, journalists, and relatives. Even the church made one last attempt to reclaim his soul, but he would not budge. He pleaded to be left in peace, and he found it hard to believe that they did still not understand that even when one is face to face with death, two and two still make four. Halfway through his life in Arzamus he had encountered the "death that should not be." Now, forty-one years later, it was the time.

Sired by the Russian folk-soul, Leo Tolstoy's destiny was synchronized to its revolution. The national adrenalin surging through his veins also energized other revolutionaries. But some of those were subverted by materialism. Both streams— the moral and the materialistic—were fed from the same source, but Tolstoy's was cleansed and ennobled by his Christian compassion. He sought to heal the suffering masses by awakening a conscience which would not resist evil with force but redeem it through love. He cried for a moral revolution, while others swept the fields with terror.

Souls who are ahead of their time, who wrestle to implement the inspiration which will eventually change the mind and heart of humankind, seem to be irradiated by the white incandescence cast by the spirit of the age. But this pure light has to penetrate many instinctual and mental layers before it can illuminate the soul and motivate action. Its pristine radiance, therefore, becomes colored, even muddied when it encounters the resistance of human nature. All of us are living contradictions, incongruous compounds of lead and gold. In fact, such powerful contradictions can be the source of immense forces of creativity. Only by destroying our illusions can we build a new identity, and in men like Dostoyevsky, Pascal, and Tolstoy it was a tortuous ordeal.

What kind of Christian was Tolstoy? Rather than an esoteric Christ, Tolstoy's was the shepherd who exemplified love, sacrifice, and service. Had Tolstoy lived in Palestine two thousand years ago, he might well have found himself among the shepherds on the winter plains. He would not have followed the Star of the Magi, for those wise men read Christ in the heavens, while the shepherds heard Him in their hearts. He would have seen the Jesus-child as the healer of human souls, not as the divinity found in cosmic mysteries. He looked for the spirit within—not in the processes of the world.

Tolstoy compelled himself to learn the way of the simple shepherd and respond to the proclamation "Good will to all men." He could do this only by transforming his basic desires into a love which could direct his heart, mind, and will to the good and true. Christ said, "If any man will come after me let him first deny himself," but a man cannot deny himself unless he has already found himself; he cannot sacrifice that which he does not yet possess. That was Tolstoy's way. Only when he had discovered the devotional-feminine in himself, was he ready to give, to lose himself. Early in his life, he absorbed the Sermon on the Mount, which inspired his approach to the moral problems of self, family, and society. Although he by destiny overlooked the cosmic, the esoteric content of the Gospels, the wise rhythms of the cosmos did not fail him. They circled in the measure of his time, bringing forth his great novels one by one.

5

Fate, Freedom, and Destiny

"Destiny is the result of two factors which grow together in the life of a human being; one streams outward from the inner depths of the soul; the other comes to meet man from the world around him."
—Rudolf Steiner

I have suggested that our voyage across the ocean of time is charted by the spiritual-psychic nucleus of our being, arranging the placement of particular experiences at specific times. The time-organism monitors our acquisition of experience, and also its transmutation and incorporation into substance of being—who we are. It is the regulator of our time life, *never* the creator of experience. Having said this, we are compelled to confront the confusion arising from the idea of viewing biography as an enigmatic mixture of fate, destiny, and freedom. How exactly are these three elements involved in the construction of biography?

Fatalists insist that biography is engineered by chromosomes, environments, or the inscrutable will of God. This view
leaves no room for any kind of free genesis in the psychic levels of individuality. Essentially, all three are mechanistic
assumptions, leaving the dubious self as a powerless victim of
circumstance, capable only of blaming everything for its misfortunes—except itself!

On the one hand, I appear to make decisions with my rational
mind in apparent freedom based on all the available information I can muster; on the other, a glance at the sequential patterns in my biography discloses an overall plan unfolding in
time and space, more or less unconsciously. In retrospect, I
would not have chosen the suffering and hardship that has
shaped me. I would probably have taken the path of least resistance. Can we get beyond this paradox? The problem boils
down to the quality of the word "choice." Shall I accept that job
offer, or not? My eventual decision, implemented by my will,
will construct a chain of mostly unpredictable experiences. A
"no" would unfold a different course. So which line of experience do I really need? Does it matter anyway?

We will examine these questions later by looking at the role
of consciousness in decision-making. In the meantime, let us
put the problem in its most elementary terms. Many folk would
agree, looking back over their paths, that their biographies were
largely constructed by an undefinable inner drive, a hungry
quest for experience which appears to be, outrageously, more
unconscious than conscious—personal development by sleep-
walking. What makes fate and freedom so enigmatic is the vast
divide between the waking mind and the unconscious regions of
the self. By converting experience into consciousness, however,
we gradually fashion a bridge between the two. The unconscious part of our being may know what reality is, but limited
rational minds only glimpse tiny splinters of it. The great seers
are unanimous in the view that a conscious penetration of the

core of our personal reality will uncover the self's full connection to world and universe. Hence, the degree of freedom depends on the level of consciousness.

Experience, then, whether rationally chosen or not, is the vital connection between the growing self and the world. In a sense, our frail little earthly ego stands on the edge of a limitless inland sea of unconsciousness while facing the external world. It stands in a region indicative of the marginal world of unrest between sea and land, a region ever changing, mingling, shifting, reforming. From this position, it is difficult to find any firm bedrock of certainty. One way, however, we can begin to relate experience to the mysteries of fate, freedom, and destiny is to trace their roles in the evolving consciousness of humankind.

The Historical Path from Fate to Freedom

History illuminates the climb from unconsciousness to consciousness. This path is reflected also in the changing attitudes to fate and freedom. The ancient mind was completely dominated by fate, personal destiny was strictly subordinate to the greater destiny of its tribal society and to the gods. In fact, our ancient forebears greatly feared the ominous presence of the "Fates," often symbolized by three sisters.

Homer, for instance, speaks of the three *Morai*—Clotho, who spins the threads of life, Lachesis, who casts the lots, and Atropos, bringer of the inevitable. These *Morai* belonged to the dynasty of Chronos-Saturn. Remember, even above mighty Zeus there hovered the supreme Chronos power of *Moros* (destiny). Plato also mentions this triad, but in the form of Atropos, the Inevitable; Ananke, Necessity; and Adrastreia, the Inescapable. Similarly, the Romans honored Fortuna and the birth goddesses called *Parcae*. In Scandinavia, these dark mistresses of fate were called *Norns*: Urd, Coming into Being; Skuld, Creation; and

Verdand, Settlement. Learned in the old customs, they judged the fate each person merited, and not only the Scandinavians but all the Germanic peoples feared their powers. Even the mighty Aesir gods of Norse mythology could no more escape their fate than the humble men of Midgard.

The dreamlike mentality of the early civilizations was supported and nourished by their highly ritualized participation in the union of group, nation, nature, and cosmos. The individual, whether high priest or slave, was a "victim" of fate, compelled to align self-will with the dictates and ministrations of the gods, initiates, and tribal law. If the group failed to obey, it incurred the wrath of its divine mentors, who sent pestilence, famine, or war to chastise it. If the tribe took up its weapons, the individual followed: if it suffered defeat, he submitted. Thus, fate decreed all. Born into a prescribed bloodline at the appointed place and time, the individual was shadowed by powers who determined the number of earthly days. The feeling of personal freedom, in the modern sense, remained in a larval stage, while the priests and initiates were charged with the spiritual responsibility of protecting this slow gestation of consciousness.

Inevitably, this attitude to fate changed when the old orders of society dissolved, thus weakening the dreamlike subservience to the gods. The individual became increasingly aware of the cut-and-dried world of cause and effect from the self- and sense-centered point of view. Disrobed of innocence and armed with a waking sense of independence, human heroes dared to challenge the old gods and their restrictions. The Mesopotamian hero, Gilgamesh, for example, braving the wrath of Ishtar, demanded the right to search for the meaning of life and death. Indeed, throughout the length and breadth of mythogenesis, this awakening spirit of independence caused much commotion in celestial quarters.

The unique consciousness of Greece added another milestone to the road to freedom. Born from the forehead of Zeus, Athena became the protector of heroes and cities. With the owl as her symbol, she presided over the emerging intellect of Athens, inspiring its search for wisdom—not the oracle wisdom, but the first stage of *independent thinking*. And Apollo charged human beings to know themselves. Thus, the lustrous fame of Athens arose from independent minds experimenting with discussion, argument, philosophical inquiry, and representative government, while the old gods reluctantly withdrew to Olympus to watch and quarrel over their rebellious subjects. They had been doomed the moment the human mind turned its eyes downward to the natural world and inward into human nature. Henceforth, the new gods would be called science, history, psychology, and philosophy. The Greeks chose to relegate their gods to second-ary regions, preferring instead to listen to the whispers of their own souls. Like Oedipus, they ignored the furious goddesses of fate in favor of a fresh new impulse—*conscience*.

Likewise, the Roman gods were relegated to less involved roles, although fate lingered on in the guise of omens and augu-ries. Despite the rumblings of independent thinking and the rise of personality, however, the destiny of the individual was strictly subservient to the destiny of Rome. But, as Franz Cumont points out, the Romans noticed the inconsistencies in the old beliefs. He mentions Suetonius, who noted that Tiberius was so con-vinced that everything was ruled by fate that he neglected the practice of his religion. Alexander of Aphrodisias was another who remarked on the strange logic of those who regarded fate as being fixed, while imploring the gods to change it!

This movement from fate toward liberty is also reflected in biblical evolution. In the Old Testament, the severe hand of Jahweh administered rewards and punitive measures to a peo-ple ruled by their sharply delineated group-consciousness. Whenever they stepped out of line with the Mosaic law of development, catastrophes chastened and awakened them to their appointed mission. Jahweh's retribution, moreover, was mirrored in the Hebrew law of fate—an eye for an eye. The function of this punishment, this "reflection," was to confront "sinners" with the consequences of their actions, thus raising their consciousness and realigning their subservience to the ordained destiny of the people.

The advent of Christianity offered humankind a completely new path to freedom. The Christ, by uniting His destiny with the destiny-potential of every individual, shattered the bonds of the old blood ties, caste systems, and racial superiorities. Of course, every soul remained responsible for its own actions—that much of the old fate remained. But Christ extolled a path of development founded on a higher level of self-awareness, enriched by an evolving conscience and compassion—a path leading to the union of soul and spirit.

We now have the potential to advance to a level of loving the divine in perfect freedom rather than in obedience to moral duty or nasty threats to our immortality. A more profound, unpossessive, unconditional connection to our neighbors is now possible. Love, then, becomes a creative, consciousness-raising, healing, cohesive force in human destiny. Such a higher quality of love recognizes the spiritual reality of others and relishes and sanctifies their freedom. Furthermore, we are free, through love, to forgive those who injure us, although still compelled to confront our own errors generated by our compulsions, fears, instincts, and reactions. Thus, fate "happens" to us when we act without a higher form of moral awareness, but vanishes altogether when we take supraconscious control over our decision making. Developing this for ourselves gives us a true choice between fate and freedom. Love, which has always provided the inherent momentum within evolution, now becomes consciously and morally expressed through the self-directed will.

Christ's deed on Golgotha and the Sermon on the Mount completely and irrevocably altered and elevated the spiritual transaction between human beings and the divine, and between individual and individual. By forgiving those who trespass against us, the obsolete laws of fate no longer demand that we return like with like to arouse consciousness. By no means does this idea suggest mere passive acceptance. On the contrary, it is an immensely creative deed of freedom touching the very roots of the other's psyche. Thus, forgiveness is a supreme act of freedom rather than fate—an incredible force of destiny-redemption.

Christianity injected its freedom-provoking impulse into human consciousness, but morality became institutionalized by the obdurate interpretations of theologians as the Church extended its authority. Consequently, consciousness was disciplined by professional moralists while fate was extended to the afterlife. Eternal damnation or the bounty of heaven depended on how one's conduct conformed to the rules. Although the soul of the age was encased in this protective cocoon of faith, its mental expansion continued unabashed, thus ensuring the separation of faith and reason, and, with it, the widening schism between soul and spirit. The medieval soul remained the property of the Church but the irrepressible sense of liberty inspired the exploration of new lands and ideas, and mastery of the provisional world. So, despite its awesome power, the Church felt compelled to fight for the rights of the soul and its sacramental needs. It did so in two ways: first, by brutally enforcing conformity, second, by entering the arena of intellectual argument.

But the analytical cat was out of the ecclesiastical bag. The method of discovery had itself been discovered, and nothing could stifle the eureka's of Copernicus, Galileo, and Newton. What remained of mythic unity splintered into diverse sciences as the growing sense of liberty was bewitched by ideas of development, progress, and exploitation. The biblical notion of dominion had reached the intellect, and there was no holding it back. Interest in eternal destiny was eclipsed by an enthralling preoccupation with the mortal life span. This new sense of liberty turned to batter the very fortresses of tradition built to protect the slumbering ego. It was this "change of mind" that precipitated the Reformation, and the French, American, and Industrial Revolutions.

Despite the new mind at large, fate was not about to let go without a fight. It now disguised itself as duty, nationalism, and scientific determinism. By subduing and harnessing nature, we have emancipated ourselves from it, thus gaining a measure of independence. The mechanistic view of life, so prevalent today, ripped us from the womb of the spiritual universe, but also sensitized our perception of our own uniqueness and right to a reasonable degree of personal liberty.

The intellectual knowledge and prosperity wrought by science and technology permits us a better chance of pursuing our goals—if only we knew them. Despite the numerous institutions designed to protect individual liberty, the true meaning of freedom remains as elusive as ever. Many people now begin to realize that higher forms of freedom do not exist in ingenious social systems, scientific utopias, or dogmatic theologies, but are rooted in the interior life of the individual seeking self-mastery through self-knowledge.

By and large, the miraculous plasma once energizing the mind and will of the age of exploration and industrial revolution has steadily lost touch with the immense potential of the human heart. Everywhere we see disquieting signs of the loss of drive, the loss of soul—and a terrifying pessimism and loneliness. The rise of independent thought, morality, and action has brought with it an acute sense of isolation. Indeed, the wake of liberty is strewn with unexpected dangers, the violence of desperation, a rising suicide rate, moral confusion, escapes into tranquilized consciousness, the regressive drift into the collective mind of ideologies. Obviously, by discarding the crutches of tradition, we have exposed ourselves to the frightening psychological pressures of the modern world.

Cause and Effect

It is obvious by now that any genuine understanding of fate, destiny, and freedom can be uncovered only if we penetrate the essential reality of human nature. As a youth swept up in the flush of brilliant scientific achievements, I naively assumed science would disclose the meaning of human existence, and restore the glorious harmony of the world. My early enthusiasm ignored the fact that science merely catalogs and manipulates the stuff of the universe. Any personal relationship to it must be left to other modes of enlightenment.

Rational thinking has tutored our observational skills, but is perilously incapable of answering questions about freedom and reality. If the universe is nothing more than the machine of scientific determinism, then all is fate, since robots run on fate not freedom. Of course, we invented a psychology to explore our interior world, but, despite the initial euphoria, it adopts the selfsame rationale as mechanistic science. Even for science, the laws of cause and effect are in dire need of repair; for a true understanding of human nature, they are flagrantly inept.

There is a world of difference between the ancient mythological perception of cause and effect and the current view inherent in scientific method. The ancients beheld a cosmos teeming with spiritual beings and forces involved in human evolution. The modern mind, on the other hand, conceptualizes a universe operating under physical laws. In fact, these laws of cause and effect give science its respectability. Without calculable laws, any uniformity in the world's behavior in time is unintelligible, and an empirical route to concepts is impossible. Without the provisional world's predictability, scientists would be forced to choose a different profession. A simple example should suffice: We can calculate our distance from a thunderstorm by counting the seconds between flash and crash, since light and sound travel at predictable velocities. If they failed to move at reliable rates, we could not use them for measurement.

Even so, the contradictions and irregularities daily appearing at the frontiers of knowledge force science on the defensive. We hear much more of the "probable result" these days—definitely more humble and tolerant. Outgrowing its Newtonian childhood and Einsteinian adolescence, science now encounters the edge of the paranormal world—one scorning the old laws. Only a new view of cause and effect, an emancipated attitude to human nature and time, can ever hope to penetrate these mysteries, particularly the secrets of life and consciousness. Few now in the modern world would dispute the fact that the human psyche obeys an entirely different order of laws.

The mechanists design magnificent mathematical models of the universe, but human nature always insists on hurling a monkey wrench into them. If, indeed, the universe is a machine, there can be no place for free individuality, no good or evil, only inevitability. There can be no choice, or justice, and no room for independent uniqueness, eccentricity, or free will. Furthermore, if this kind of fate is valid, we cannot be held accountable for our own actions.

Although our physicality and basic instincts are interconnected with nature, we contain something uniquely special which elevates us above and beyond it. The human ego, the I, makes us supranatural beings. Evolution demands that we transform the laws of nature in us to promote our ascent toward individuality and freedom, thus clearing a space for the psyche and harnessing its potential powers. To do this, we have to suppress and arrest the influence of nature. Thus, the evolution of selfhood is a process of slowly rejecting the external world to fashion a center for the psyche's *own causality*. Had we remained prisoners of nature, we would never be more than mechanical-biochemical, egoless robots incapable of free will. This grotesque image reminds us of the "Darwinian human being," molded by heredity and environment, and driven by a primal instinct for survival.

A quick glance at the animal kingdom confirms the connection between freedom and centric consciousness. On the lowest levels, the humble termite, like ant and bee, is totally subordinate to the colony as a whole. The queen exhibits a small degree of autonomy but is also subservient to the biogenic laws of her species. In fact, all the activity of creature and colony is devoted to its biological format; nothing remains for the development of higher faculties. The colony is ruled by fate, by genetic causality.

The lion, standing higher on the scale of complexity, reveals a greater measure of mobility, virtuosity, and independence. Though still dominated by instinct, the lion shows signs of temperament and emotion. I have met volatile, as well as lazy or placid lions. Even so, this magnificent creature is still fated to obey the instinctual code of its species. This collective, highly specialized nature of the lion cannot accommodate an independent self, since it is compelled to obey the laws of its group soul. This collective instinct is the root of lion causality and fate. The fact that it must *learn* to use its instincts through *play*, places it higher on the scale that leads to freedom.

The ape is even higher. As biological activity is repressed, so inwardness and independence increase—a fundamental law of life. The benefits of consciousness are gained at the expense of biological power and the forces of repair and renewal. A starfish can grow a new limb but lacks the vanity to admire it, while the ape cannot regenerate a limb, but is endowed with rudimentary mental abilities. The more conscious nature becomes, the less biological vitality it possesses. Consciousness brings vulnerability, but vulnerability is compensated by increased intelligence.

The primates approach the physical characteristics and instincts of Homo sapiens, but despite the considerable increase in dexterity and the ability to exploit experience, the instinctual life of the tribe prevents the full appearance of an individual ego. Apes, with a degree of versatility unknown to species below theirs, are nevertheless imprisoned by their instinctual tribal patterning. Although bearing a human resemblance, the ape has become a fixed idea; it is too rigid, too specialized, too finished. Despite its psychological potential, the ape is denied the experience of humanhood since its physical and sentient equipment is simply not pliable enough to sustain an independent ego.

The ape matures rapidly, while we take our time. This is why we are so vulnerable in our early life. By *retarding* our development, we remain unspecialized and pliable enough to permit the progressive integration of an independent ego—a spiritual nucleus. The ape is born with its milk teeth, receives its second teeth by the third year, and is sexually functional by the fifth or sixth year. Its facial features, amazingly humanlike in the young embryo, become wizened long before birth. True, it begins to lift its spine into a vertical position, but the attempt is inconclusive; its partially free arms and hands give it much more mobility, but its behavior has to conform to the codes of tribal conduct. Compared to humans, the ape is drastically aged and has little psychic power available for the development of higher faculties such as conscience, morality, and advanced conceptual thinking.

Human nature can sink into animality, but animals cannot rise to egohood. Only an ego can write a sonnet or invent a hydrogen bomb. Ape life and fate are conditioned by tribal law rooted in instinct, but Homo sapiens, using thought, devises totally unworkable social systems—and then lampoons them! The difference is the level of self-consciousness. Yet conventional science insists that humans are nothing but highly refined genetic complexes, like the ape. It ignores the spiritual identity of the independent human self. This is in sharp contrast to the spiritual view which perceives the Self as being both the selector and the transformer of heredity and environment; the Ego is the primary source of human causality. Orthodox science recognizes fate, but is ill-equipped to face the mystery of freedom and destiny.

The staggering expansion of genetic engineering has brought with it immensely serious ethical questions. If human beings deliberately manipulate genetic structures, altering human heredity by using relatively superficial rational thought, then only perfect genetic structures would be acceptable. Race and individual would be judged solely on their genetic efficiency. Only the genetic elite would inherit the earth, and Hitler sinned by being born a century too early.

These two streams of opposed mentality, becoming clearly more divergent by the day, represent the great divide facing human potential. Mechanistic genetics is sheer fate. The spiritual perception of evolution, on the other hand, believes the genetic fabric of physical life is designed to present the evolving individual with the resistances *promoting* the challenge of self-transformation—the conversion of suffering into consciousness. Thus, this self-evolution converts fate into freedom. Furthermore, this view stresses the pivotal point that each Self *selects* its genetic constitution with an interior wisdom infinitely more profound than that achieved by the rational intellect.

Having reached this point, we can now take the problem of cause and effect further by looking for signs of fate and freedom in the way we conjure up decisions.

Consciousness and Decision-Making

"Every cause is the effect of its own effects."
—Ibn 'Arabi

The remorseless drive of evolution engineered the awakening of the kind of consciousness responsible for the growing interest in human rights. This emergence is reflected in humankind's increasing use of its ability to think as separate individuals. The stronger the sense of Self became, the more individuals felt responsible for their own choice of action. Conversely, the more primitive the thought life, the more collectively dependent were the people. Obviously, the degree of self-awareness decides whether the process of cause and effect is ruled by fate or freedom.

My decision to work in the United States was one of a complex series of apparently free choices shaped by a mixture of ideals, the quest for experience, and available opportunities. Subsequently, that particular choice conducted me onto a line of events, some of them bringing success, some not, some bringing great joy, others deep sorrow. Had I anticipated the painful consequences, I would have tried to avoid them. Looking back over my track of "free" choices, I am now aware of their inevitability rather than true freedom. Each decision triggered new events, which in turn demanded new decisions, and so on. Similarly, my first cause was intimately connected to earlier decisions; in fact, I can trace this line of causality all the way back to my birth! In retrospect, I detect the approximate design of my biographical path, but I was unconscious of it in all the "nows" when my judgements and actions were taken. It looks as if mostly fate rather than freedom held the helm of my ship. Obvious too, is the fact that my paucity of insight inhibited my full use of experience. A stronger consciousness and more self-knowledge would have heightened my appreciation of the implications and consequences of my decisions. I would have kneaded the dough of experience more thoughtfully, better appreciated my joys and sorrows, better learned my lessons, tied loose ends, left less undone. Presumably, the subsequent acts would have been more fulfilling, my path more direct and more helpful to those sharing each stage of my drama.

How free were my decisions? Were some of them engineered somewhere in my unconscious self by some manner of psychic causation? What is the true source of the process by which we make our major decisions? After all, the idea that the masterwork of biography is, to some degree, the result of a predetermined plan implies that some of our decisions, though apparently chosen by the waking mind, actually spring from the very core of our being. Perhaps, for example, to oblige a friend, you decided to attend a party despite tiredness or disinterest. In spite of reluctance and rational excuses, *something* in you made you relent. But this apparently trivial decision altered the course of your life when you met the person whom you fell in love with and later married. Thus, your original decision shifted you from the path you would have followed had you stayed at home to the one now revealed by your biography. You were certainly free to refuse the invitation, so where did the "yes" really come from when your waking mind preferred to say "no"? Did you *have* to go? To trace your decision down into the subliminal layers of the self where it may have been generated, demands a perception and cognition far in advance of your normal thinking.

Obviously, the more conscious we are of our motives and their consequences, the more free our decisions become. This is plain to see when we compare carefully contemplated decisions with those based solely on instinct or emotion. This means we can postulate an ascending scale of freedom, a ladder of consciousness, or better, *thoughtfulness*. At the bottom, thought is indistinguishable from instinct, habit, appetite, etc. Further along, we come to the decisions swayed by feelings. Then we reach a level where thought can analyze, judge, and anticipate—where we carefully work out our decisions. We use this kind of analytical thinking to do crossword puzzles or, if we are gifted, to evaluate statistics, ponder philosophical arguments, or design computers. Intellectual judgements which can identify our motives are certainly freer than emotional ones, but have we reached the top end of the scale?

Evolution has remorselessly raised the anthropos out of its blissful symbiosis to the stage of experiencing its point-centered awareness of personality and individuality. This much-lauded degree of intellection which employs the senses to explore and evaluate the external world also perceives the surface ruminations of the psyche. But this is but a pallid semblance of our true reality, say the great seers. We can of course be justly proud of our hard-won, though, at times, discomforting sense of self, the ego invested in our rational thinking. But this rational mind, so glorified by Descartes, is merely another rung on the ladder of ascending awareness. The seers declare it dull and palely loitering with intent compared to the quality of thinking and pellucid perception attainable by embarking on a path of inner development through our own efforts. The old rational mind has exploited the resources of nature, but now it is time to exploit the dormant resources of the psyche. Despite the colossal achievements of our cerebral civilization, we are aware of something else, a deep-seated longing to uncover the full reality of being an individual. We know we are more than we seem, behind the veils of rational intelligence.

The true seers, those pathfinders of new perception, insist we are within reach of an insight incomparably higher, richer, purer, which can pour itself into the shell, that preliminary ego vessel we call the waking ego. This crowning self, the high ego, the God within, call it what you will, is nothing less than the full magnificence of our spiritual reality recoverable through our own efforts. The seers' extensive and intensive discipline and training achieves new levels of humanhood, new regions of freedom. They are able to spiritualize the intellect, and awaken those dormant organs of perception which lead to the union of soul and spirit. It is a magnificent vision.

To survey the scale of ascending thoughtfulness, let us take four simplified examples illustrating the connection between thought and decision making. The first is someone half asleep at the wheel of a car which drifts into the path of an oncoming truck. Instantly the person thinks, or more correctly, *reacts* to avoid a collision. This decision is instinctive since the driver had no time to think out a solution. Perception and action are almost instantaneous.

The second case is a suicidal person deliberately choosing to make an "accident" happen by driving into a wall. More than likely this person has wrestled with thoughts on life and death for some time, but anguish inundates the psyche and obscures clear thinking; it is the pain, the emotion that grasps for deliverance.

The third example, like the second, is a person who is tortured by mental and emotional anguish, and is also tempted to end it all, but whose reasoning is resilient enough to ride out the storms, and who may be swayed by family responsibilities or, perhaps, belief or conscience offered by a religion. Whatever the case, reason or faith triumphs over self-destructive impulses—thought, not emotion, is the overseer.

The final example is a seer carrying immeasurable burdens of spiritual pain, but who, unlike the others, possesses the spiritual power to examine predicaments with a rare degree of self knowledge and spiritual insight. Aware of the immortal consequences of actions, this person would never jeopardize the future by choosing suicide. The seer *knows* the purpose of suffering and freely chooses to accept travail, accepting the wisdom of life and approaching every action with moral clarity.

In all four cases, thought was present but in differing, ascending stages of freedom. The first was based on instinct, the second on emotion, the third on a mixture of logic and faith, the fourth on direct spiritual knowledge.

Compared with the seer's enlightened cognition, the orthodox mind blunders about in a daydream. The seer is aligned to destiny. But what about those of us groping around for a path while lugging our heavy mix of childhood dysfunctions, ancient angers, experience, analysis, logic, and faith, even an ideal or two thrown in for good measure? Assuming we do have a personal mission, we certainly make heavy weather of it. What happens if we make erroneous decisions? Every new decision contains a trace of its ancestry. Each is a cause and also an effect. Does one false move mean that they are all erroneous? Are we on a definite course or on countless mini routes going every which way? If the psyche holds an ideal itinerary in the depths of its wisdom, how on earth can we remain true to something we cannot fathom with the rational mind?

Perhaps there may be a few resemblances between actual and ideal paths, but we take false turns, meet dead ends, take the long way round. Pretty depressing, is it not? It should not be if we picture the psyche as a dynamic, never static engine of transformation ever ready to adjust and chart a new course. The course is ever changeable, but the destination is not. Destiny changes with every new experience. In fact, any serious study of biography worthy of the name drives home the point that we more often than not make the correct decisions for the wrong reasons. One person may unconsciously "choose" an illness, another may blindly create one through a negligent life style. The illness is an event designed to readjust the course—it was not in the primary plan. Fate, indeed, is ever willing to furnish the sleepwalker with consciousness-raising obstacles. We call this adjustment a "crisis."

The surface mind may think it is on the right course, but the astonishing synchrony of events has a nasty habit of intruding to effect a necessary change of course. The ordinary mind makes decisions based on the best available information but is barely aware of the true reasons. This is why we can make the right destiny decisions for the wrong reasons. For example, we may select a job for financial or career reasons, only to find unexpected failures and suffering. The real goal was the painful experiences. Seen in this light, failure is invaluable, and our enemies are our servants of change and opportunity.

No matter what the level of consciousness and proportions of fate or freedom, one can always detect the presence of an irrepressible wisdom at the helm of biography. But most of us totter along, dependent on our resident direction finder, the I, weighed down by its cargo of unfreedom. There are times when we feel becalmed with a deserted horizon bereft of the smallest sail of opportunity. We should realize, however, that experience must be transformed before new impulses and directives well up into consciousness. The psyche must obey its rhythms; all the impatience in the world cannot intimidate the cycles of transformation. No matter what the surface phenomena of our existence, the psyche faithfully prepares new opportunities and a stage for synchrony to create new connections.

The enlightened ones standing on the higher escarpments of consciousness are unequivocally committed to destiny, knowing the path to be traversed. They have an aerial view of it, while our vision is partially blocked by the local obstructions of personality, old patterns, and ingrained methods of perception. Since the seers' deepest psychic substratum is accessible to perception, they can translate its motives into morally imbued deeds, never staggering or cavorting along the track, never mere reactors to events. Thus they are conscious creators of destiny, truly and fully committed to the spiritual goals of personal and cosmic evolution. Having transmuted the past, they are free to receive the future, aligning the full force of heart, mind, and will to destiny—with immense composure. No matter what persecutions befall them, no one can steal their freedom; they can be perfectly free in a concentration camp. They guard their thoughts with great diligence, knowing full well that thoughts spread into both inner and outer worlds like diffracting ripples on a pond. Such true individuals are the conscious masters of their own causality, standing before us like beacons. Their faculties are actively developed, while ours lie mostly dormant. The essential contrast between our fate and their freedom is the creative power of their thinking invested with the energizing presence of heart and will.

Consciousness being the key to freedom, I would urge the reader to examine Rudolf Steiner's major contribution, *The Philosophy of Freedom*. This epochal work provides us with the opportunity to investigate and make personal a whole new approach to cognition and freedom.

The Eternal Cause

"Free decisions are governed by the immortal part of man." —Rudolf Steiner

Destiny is a relentless and irrepressible force within the psyche regardless of the level of consciousness. In terms of biography, what we lack in freedom we gain through *necessity*. This imperative to mature through experience is the driving force inherent in all human biography, compelling one person to explore Antarctica, another to devote a lifetime to repairing shoes; it transforms a paperboy into a movie mogul, an astronaut into a humble priest. The goal of all destiny is evolution through self-transformation, but life is brief and triumphs are few. Rapid advancement is highly improbable for many and impossible for some. And there's the rub.

No matter how diligently we strive to deepen consciousness and transform our lives, we know we will not approach the glorious freedom extolled by the seers by the time we die. Are we then to be numbered among the lamentable, among the millions of rejects assigned a lesser role in the universal plan? Not only would that make a maniacal parody of our own sense of quest and of the struggles of our loved ones, but the unbounded suffering of the world would be nothing more than a preposterous scandal, a useless mess of grotesqueries signifying nothing. As yet, we have added but a little to life—yet we could die tomorrow! Are we not over and over again confounded by the disturbing discrepancy between the sublime intellectual, spiritual, and emotional potential of the human soul, and the all-too-obvious fallibility of the physical body? How then can we give credence to the idea of life as a path of personal development if this one brief flit through mortality is all there is?

Surely, biography must amount to more than one meager chip of mortal experience; such a solitary camp on the long trek to fulfillment cannot itself reveal the sovereign meaning and full extent of destiny. If mortal life is to have meaning as a vessel for development, there must be a personal existence both before and after the narrow time slice of a single life span. If destiny is self-designed, only a penetrative understanding of its immortal character unfolds a screen wide enough to envision the complete picture of its meaning. The true purpose of destiny as a suprapersonal means of evolution must be concealed somewhere in the mystery of our *immortality.*

The great religions acknowledge the immortality of the human spirit and discuss the afterlife, although they are deafeningly silent on our celestial whereabouts before birth. This is rather odd since there cannot be fragments of immortality, only levels or stages in its perpetuity. So perhaps it would be more helpful if we ignored the established doctrines for the moment and returned to the old dilemmas of cause and effect.

Take, for example, a teacher about to demonstrate cause and effect by propelling one billiard ball toward another. The teacher insists that if all the elements of force, friction, speed, mass, weight, and angle are known, the direction, speed, and distance the second ball will travel can be confidently predicted; the result depends on the operation of strictly mechanical laws. But this is only one way of looking at it. We could remind the teacher that the effect is also the cause! It is the result, the effect, the future goal of the demonstration that actually initiates decision and action. Not only does the idea exist before the ball is struck, it is the future directly influencing the present. Of course, if the ball is not hit correctly, the effects will not accord with the goal: what was possible will not become actualized since the execution is the crucial factor. Now let us apply this idea to destiny.

I have suggested that the I is the true bearer of the causation behind the genesis of biography—a causality generating first the cause, then the effects. But we can just as well reverse this, as with the billiard ball. We can imagine the goals embedded in the future motivating our present actions, simultaneously adjusting to the results of our past experience. Thus the primary goals of destiny drawing us ever onward exist actually within past, present, and future—they live in the all-at-once time.

But where is the freedom? The goals of earthly destiny are self-chosen, but the waking mind is free to be sidetracked depending on the strength of its intellectual, emotional, and volitional constitution. It may fail one test but another path will be found since the self's dynamics, its intrinsic nature, compels us to seek it. Waking consciousness is free to abandon the journey or delay the departure. Time and life slip by and we may miss the boat, but the true goals remain and the I will contrive another itinerary. Perhaps the target was true but the aim faulty, nudged off track by weakness or misjudgment. Perhaps the ostensible goals conjured up by the waking mind led us into all kinds of self-transforming experience and that was the real meaning of the mission.

The body, senses, and waking mind are anchored in linear time judging everything in terms of past, present, and future. But the core of our causal reality lives in *unbounded time*. Destiny however, is compelled to unfold as a process in *linear time*. This is the earth's greatest spiritual asset, its greatest virtue—to be the place where the eternal transforms the temporal. If personal destiny and immortality are dual expressions of the same mystery, we will never fully decode the mysteries of biography by scanning but one mortal life span, one brief stanza in the eternal epic of our wholeness.

Without this overview, life appears swamped by injustice and meaninglessness wherever we look. If the mission of life is to find fulfillment, what chance is there for the baby who lives but a few hours, or the young man drafted to a battlefield grave? Where is the justice? Where is the fulfillment? Why should some stand at the very frontiers of new consciousness while others, locked in primitive cultures, appear to be orphans of evolution? Why should we experience the exceptional dilemmas of this century while others sleep in the anonymous tombs of antiquity? Yes, it is impossible to measure justice in terms of one finite span of passing time. Only by taking immortality as a frame of reference can we begin to envision a transcendental justice based on higher laws. A biography of an hour or of a hundred years is a mere flicker in the eye of time compared with the span of civilizations and cosmic aeons.

Rather we should imagine each human drama as a fleeting scene on an infinite cosmic stage. Birth is a vital act of self-realization, but the child whose time is severed by early death is neither lost nor doomed since its goals survive. If the baby's self is immortal, there must be other opportunities for growth and development. If every tributary of experience feeds the mainstream of universal meaning, a baby's premature demise not only becomes part of its own creative experience but adds to the total experience of humanity and cosmos. No matter how short or wretched, a life can never be an irrelevant atom of nuisance—it never loses a scrap of its cosmic-eternal proportions. Only a view of destiny seen in the light of its cosmic heritage and continuity renders transparent the terrible masks of necessity often cursing our mortal sojourn.

What an infinite commitment of *will* each sovereign Self lavishes on the mortal self which so often behaves like a spoiled child or a cantankerous reactionary! What love! What uninhibited love-power each I invests in destiny. Surely every biography offers us a living imagination of those exalted degrees of love the divine invests in human becoming.

A true cognition of the human life span, a cognition fortified by love, strength, and healing, arises when we view destiny in terms of its cosmic accountability and continuity. To do this we must learn to examine the mystery of biography in terms of reincarnation and the laws of karma.

6

The Seasons of Immortality

"Human life can be fulfilled not only in creating and enjoying, but also in suffering."

—Victor E. Frankl, *The Doctor and the Soul*

"A wound is the beginning of every sense,
Only by pain transmuted can we perceive the world.
The wound of a heart overcome, becomes an eye,
 That sees into life, that knows, that heals."

—Eleanor Trives, *The Sun's Path*

The Brotherhood of Pain

Without a meaningful place for suffering in our personal inlook and outlook of life, we can fashion no valid philosophy of human existence. What possible justification can there be for the vast assemblage of tribulations, impediments, aches, and miseries of existence? Who among us has not angrily questioned the purpose of the anguish continually flaring and subsiding at millions of points all over this planet in distress? Surely it is impossible to discuss human destiny without attempting to comprehend the forbidding specter of pain all must encounter at one time or another. Pain is the universal ingredient in human destiny that we dare not ignore.

Suffering, whatever the variety, presents a challenge demanding a response. Not only must we experience our own pain through disease, accident, grief, humiliation, guilt, and the blows of malice, we cannot isolate ourselves from the agony of a world gripped by conflict and want. Pain is the great equalizer and every soul bears its mark. We can turn a blind eye, drug ourselves with pleasures, or hide behind barricades of security, but we cannot ignore or escape its consequences.

Pain is a sentient vibration passing from one to another to stir a response, be it alarm, pity, guilt, or compassion. We can never fully experience another's pain, but it nevertheless entreats us to reach out to them. Although the will to survive lies at the instinctual root of our drive for fulfillment, the self forfeits both hope and power if it fails to uncover any purpose in its travail or to be supported by care and consolation. Through the suffering of others, one's own life is enriched by meaning. Adversity draws souls together, thus weaving the rapport responsible for so many victories of spirit, so many unsung acts of heroism and service.

Why should suffering play so powerful and widespread a role in mortal life? What is its significance for our personal development? Did we sow its seeds in a previous existence? If so, what fruit will it bear in the future? One way we can sense the value of pain is by viewing it as a catalyst, an agent of change and transformation. Paradoxically, the pain of neighbors draws us toward them, but our own hurls us back upon ourselves. Suffering is an *inhalation* which concentrates our attention. When we feel pain, we know something is wrong, our balance is upset, we are unstuck, dislodged, disordered;

something in body or soul cries out for attention. Pain we obey. Pain is a message from within. "God whispers to us in our pleasure, speaks to us in our conscience, but shouts in our pains: it is His megaphone to rouse a deaf world," said C.S. Lewis in *The Problem of Pain.*

A collision with pain halts us in our tracks. Whether skating on surfaces of superficiality, dozing in a haze of apathy, hiding in safe isolation, or charging on regardless, a sudden detonation of pain jams us into the urgency of the immediate present. Destiny mysteriously provides the hindrance, the *resistance* compelling the soul to face itself. When as children we fall off a tricycle we learn to separate ourselves from the world. Our nerve ends tell us where we end and the world begins. The laws of nature do not adjust to our demands—we bounce off them, turned back upon ourselves. Thus, collision incites consciousness.

Naturally we invite disaster by transgressing the laws of the physical world, but what about the inner laws of the soul? Are we not also hammered into reflection, recognition, and correction by failure, conflict, humiliation, and grief? Whatever the cause, the aftermath of collision stirs our mindfulness and opens a space for adjustment and self-reconstruction.

Consider, for example, the vast pool of discomfort formed by commonplace ailments such as asthma and migraine, which circle time and time again to beleaguer those predisposed and intrude upon their liberty. What is the purpose of such miseries? Do they belong to destiny? Obviously, there are biological and hereditary determinants, subtle imbalances in the body chemistry which tend to make us susceptible to certain illnesses. But accepting the physiological basis of an illness should not deter us from asking if and why we might have "chosen" these aggravating challenges.

The true mission of an illness, supposing we approve the word "mission," lies in the subtle rapport between the asthmatic's physiology and his psyche. Asthmatics inhale more or less normally but struggle to exhale. There are good medical reasons to assume that they not only tend to be allergic to certain proteins, but also have difficulties inhaling and digesting physical and social atmospheres. Their problem, primarily one of assimilation, suggests that the interaction between person and environment, between inner and outer worlds, needs attention. When we inhale we share the external world of substance through the food we eat, the air we breathe, and the thoughts, emotions, and influences of others. Not only must we fully transform our food, we must also assimilate the emotional forces arising from our relationships; we can be as allergic to emotion as we are to particles of food or dust. Asthma, in some respects, is a social imbalance—and this is the key to its function as destiny.

The problem lies in the respiration since this is where the congestion, the "damming up," occurs. If body and soul are a dynamic unity and every physical process embodies a degree of psycho-spiritual activity, then diagnosis and treatment should include both. Exhalation is a crucial component in the rhythm of life. The soul also must exhale by expressing emotion and thought through speech and action. Not only must we digest feelings about ourselves, we must also absorb those aroused by the conflicts, abuses, and pressures in our personal relationships. If the rhythm is adversely affected by too much input and not enough output, the backlog may well produce severe bronchial paroxysms in those with a sensitive respiration.

Asthma cuts its victims off from the world, a physical separation reflecting their social-emotional connection to life. Breathing, such a natural and unconscious activity, becomes a conscious act of *will*. The sufferer experiences acute restriction. Needless to say, the demoralizing fear of an impending attack tends to intensify its grip; it is yet another emotion to be dealt with. Obviously such psychosomatic ailments require more than physical solutions. The soul demands ventilation too. It would benefit adult sufferers to analyze both their connections to themselves and to their social milieu—their "social" breathing. The condition belongs to their destiny and is there to be overcome. Once this is understood, the asthma has both meaning and mission, and the sufferer will find ways to support the ego expressing itself through proper action.

Similarly, migraine can also be viewed as a form of congestion. This distressing visitation affects those with a particularly sensitive nerve-sense organization. As with the asthmatic, it is a question of overload and assimilation. The attack is both a safety valve and a warning. Too many sense impressions, anxieties, or certain substances cannot be properly assimilated; they overwhelm the psyche and force a temporary shutdown, a period of withdrawal for adjustment, for digestion. Thus asthma and migraine sufferers need to examine their relationship to life. Illness itself urges body and soul to restore the balance. Indeed, such complaints may well disappear when the psychological causation no longer exists. The impulse behind such ailments is definitely *transformative*.

Illness compels us to withdraw from the melee of daily life, thus providing an interval which has profound value for the processes of body and psyche. Those, for example, marooned in a hospital, dependent on the care of others, find themselves confined to another dimension, disconnected from normality. For many, the experience marks a decisive turning point. The shock of an operation, for example, is followed by a period of equanimity, when the mind is suspended in an altered state. It is a precious interval for serious introspection and self-recognition. Thus, suffering makes a space, a clearing in the dense forest of daily existence which prompts us to review our past, uncover buried ideals, perhaps recenter our religious feelings, and sense anew those close to us. There is nothing like the valley of the shadow to cut through habit, tedium, and complacency, forcing us to reevaluate our priorities. Thus, suffering moves us closer to ourselves, renders life more deliberate, intense, and precious—in short, it raises our awareness.

What about terminal suffering? In this case the pain is unequivocally transformative. This is the very climax of destiny, which releases one's immediate hold over loved ones, environment, and especially one's physicality. If the decline advances slowly, there are well-defined stages indicating changes in consciousness. In many cases, the reflex actions of shock, panic, anger, and rebellion are followed by resignation, then a closing stage of tranquility, as the nonphysical components of human nature disengage themselves from the corporeal. Destiny here is sheer fate. Freedom at this point depends only on the quality of the acceptance. Again, suffering is transformative and immensely so, since we move into a totally different dimension of experience and existence.

Another factor of supreme significance in the death mystery is the transformative effect it has on family and friends. Few find themselves unchanged by the experience, especially if they have shared the decline. The arrows of grief wing their way straight and true into the heart, a terrible intrusion which shatters illusions and dislocates personality as they embed themselves deep in the heartwood of our being. Like other forms of pain, grief disengages us from our environment. Although we feel stunned and inconsolable, an amazing change takes place within our cocoon of grief. Grieving itself is a growth process: first comes the shock, then the loss of bearings, perhaps anger, followed by a phase of numbness and torpor.

Such emotional pain can devastate the self, paralyze the will, vaporize all enthusiasm, and even undermine health. It can also take the form of a protracted sorrow like the pain of boredom or loneliness, a kind of subterranean leech sucking away all vitality. Obviously, it is easier to handle a broken leg than a broken heart, which can uproot the self and wreck all concentration and confidence. Such crises, themselves a sibling of death, render us unstable and vulnerable for a while.

The process, thank the psyche, moves on. Disorientation and despondency are followed by the reappearance of hope, which in time fans the glowing embers of will. The contracted soul begins to expand again as it reorders and reintegrates itself with the world. Of course, nothing can ever be the same, but we should find ourselves stronger, cleaner, and more centered. In other words, our anguish has wrought *new capacity*. Yes, grief is definitely transformative.

Naturally, the quality of the emergence depends upon the strength of the ego. Perhaps the grief overlays past untransformed trauma, unassimilated suffering. If the process is stuck, as it were, the physiological and mental stress will require treatment and the support needed to fortify the self and reintegrate it with life. For some, the grief of separation set in motion by bereavement, marital collapse, or job loss shoves them down the slippery slope into the cavernous world of depression. This form of suffering can fasten its pernicious grasp on the somatic substrate, weakening the immune system, causing a loss of vitality, sexual drive, appetite, and weight, while the overwhelmed psyche may be stricken with anxiety, agitation, delusions, even hallucinations. Being shrouded by the black drapery of depression, cut off from the higher forces of the self and renewing forces of the world, is a harrowing experience. Fortunately, modern medicine and therapeutics have begun to devote much more attention to this condition. There are encouraging signs that more significance is being given to the time-dynamics of depression, the interlaced rhythms of body, soul, and spirit. Yes, depression is clearly a transformative suffering, a real process in biographical time. It is a biographical problem, a destiny condition, part of the process of assimilating past experience. It may have chemical elements, but the real source lies much deeper.

Another example of emotional pain is the suffering of parents jolted by the blow of bearing a handicapped child. Distress grows as the seriousness of the damage becomes obvious. Parents pound themselves, asking why it should happen to them. I have known fathers who had planned the education of their children down to the last detail long before the children were born. Obviously, they have to overcome their deep resentment and disappointment. Some families regard their handicapped child as a hostile intrusion, while others lavish attention on the needy newcomer at the expense of siblings. Whatever the case, the clan has to adjust and the upheaval can wreck an unstable family or weld it together. A definitive study of the family's development will reveal just what this adjustment can mean in terms of attitudes, values, and individual development.

No one suggests the task is not a formidable one, but I have seen the handicapped child draw forth special qualities from each family member and, more than likely, expose their flaws, too. Family life acquires a different focus, often developing degrees of sacrifice, compassion, and love unknown in "normal" homes. In time, such families will admit that their handicapped child changed them for the better. Parents learn much more than the medical background associated with mental handicaps. They learn to share the delight and the significance of little things and build a relationship on attention, tolerance, and humor. Parents also learn the profound gifts of sacrifice and forgiveness despite tantrums and irrational behavior. In short, they learn to accept the defects and enjoy the compensations. Yes, this form of pain is definitely transformative.

Those who accept this challenge set for them by destiny discover that their devotion and patience are transformed into a greater capacity for giving. They also realize that their child is not a half-being, a semi-person, but an individual endowed with unique qualities, which render its extreme vulnerability a source of great influence. The Downs-syndrome child, for example, will develop only a fraction of those intellectual faculties so idolized by the modern world, but he or she often has an intensified capacity for loving and trusting, completely free from malice, suspicion, and intellectual cunning. When accepted fully, this kind of family tribulation adds new consciousness, capacity, and meaning to the destiny of each member. Is it really credible that such a "disaster" involving so many lives is merely a freak accident of nature?

But what about destiny from the standpoint of the handicapped? The first point to bear in mind is the fact that the impediments are primarily physical. Physical abnormalities prevent the psyche from freely penetrating the constricted and unresponsive body it inhabits. Is there any reason why a self equal to or even more advanced than our own could not inhabit an aberrant body for a particular destiny, a specific purpose? Destiny is twofold; it is constructed by ourselves for ourselves, but it is also an integral part of other destinies. Most handicapped persons are dependent on others for care and protection. Thus they are *compelled to trust* the world. In extreme mental handicaps, what we call "personality" will never fashion clever defensive barriers nor present artful images of itself to fool the world. They stand naked before life, immensely vulnerable yet wide open to experiences most of us miss or try to avoid.

Obviously, certain experiences will be enhanced. If the limbs, for example, are restricted in movement, just imagine the prodigious act of will needed to do the simple things we all take for granted. Or again, see how the blind are compelled to develop other areas of spatial awareness when learning to move trustingly in a world invisible to them. Just because their mental-sensory equipment is inoperable doesn't mean that handicapped people experience feelings any less intensely than we do. What pours into them from their environment is not filtered or analyzed by reason, but is experienced more or less *directly.* Theirs is not a self-creative destiny in the accepted sense, but one which has to be endured—and this is what gives it colossal spiritual meaning.

Yes, legions of handicapped add meaning to the destiny of society by arousing conscience and involvement. Their presence provokes the discomfort and compassion activating research and practical care, not to mention basic questions about the true nature of humanity and society. Could it be that we have them because we need them? From the point of view of the humanitarian energies they engender, they are an indisputable creative and productive element of society. They urge us to question our blind allegiance to a soulless materialism which regards them as an economic burden. Indeed, materialism is confounded by them. Technology can lend valuable support to their special needs, but it is those priceless intangibles, the spiritual forces of loving and caring, which make their destiny so meaningful to them and to us.

But what about the "human vegetable" in whom we detect no spark of individuality? Totally inscrutable and vulnerable, the I withdrawn to depths unknown, they have placed their selfless lives into the caring hands of others. Lying dormant in mind and body for a long period appears to be nothing more than a terrible vacuum of experience. But are they not bathed in a stream of care and attention, the thoughts, feelings, and actions of those around them? Who would dare to presume they experience nothing? Whatever the brain damage or physical and emotional deformity, the handicapped gather a veritable treasure of unique experiences between birth and death. Perhaps the real meaning of their handicaps lies buried in the subterranean regions of their unconsciousness, but this does not prevent us from wondering what creative role it plays in their immortality.

Any survey of human suffering should include what might be described as "the pain of self," perhaps the most bewildering, insidious, and resistant anguish we bear. Despite the fact that this "spiritual suffering" is also a creative, corrective force in human destiny, persons stricken with it may well crumble emotionally and then physically if it overwhelms their body chemistry. While identity crises, guilt, and humiliation are typical of this type of distress, the loss of faith suffered by priests belongs to the upper levels of the scale. Each step of their careers may well have fallen into place naturally without undue strain or upheaval, but at a certain point, inner change (perhaps triggered by an external event) precipitates the "battle with the self" which casts them into a pit of turmoil. One can find such bouts of spiritual confusion in the seven-year rhythms of such men as Tolstoy, Pascal, and Jacob Boehme. The emergence of their self-identity took the form of a tortuous series of crises triggered by psychic change.

Identity crises creep up on us from the lower levels of the psyche, but some are sparked by external events. Take the example of politicians who climb steadily to fame with the media wind of fortune at their backs. We see only their public images and the trappings of power as they stand aloof on the remote platforms of their authority; the real person is hidden. But what goes up must come down—either slowly with dignity or ingloriously at speed. The plunge may be meteoric when the wind of national destiny suddenly shifts and they suffer the disgrace and humiliation which burns away the charismatic image fashioned by their minions. When the conspiracy of events reduced Richard Nixon to human proportions, life left him humbled and demoralized to absorb his denouement and reconstruct himself as best he could. Pride, in its protean forms, distorts and magnifies our self-image, but the wisdom of growth seems to jump at the chance to bring us back to reality. To surrender oneself to compulsive change, one's self-image ripped to shreds, is undoubtedly a form of dying. But it is still transformative.

Guilt, the self-judgment of offenses against oneself or others, is another transformative form of pain. The knife that conscience twists in the gut of our being compels us to acknowledge the presence of the past in the now. It can consume confidence, lame the will, and ravage peace of mind, but it can also evoke the energy and determination to make amends. Guilt, like other forms of suffering, drives us onward by contriving to annihilate itself by corrective action. Taking the long view, it may set in motion impulses which construct our future destiny. Our longings to correct our wrongs are true formative forces that we carry into the future, even beyond death, impulses which may well express themselves somewhere in our immortal existence.

There are those who freely accept, even welcome, the opportunity of sharing the pain of others. They *deliberately* immerse their lives in the world's anguish, joyfully tending the sick, the dying, and the downtrodden. Mother Teresa and her sisters of charity are an inspiring example. Her life is uplifted and sustained by her conviction that without *sharing* the suffering, her work would be just social work; it would not be the Christ-imbued work of redemption. I have always been moved by the words Ernest Raymond applied to St. Francis: "To a man whose love was wide enough, and whose sense of unity was complete enough, the pain of the world would be a personal pain."

To sum up, we can take heart from the view that we suffer to grow and by growing we heal ourselves. This humble vantage point will help us see that the metal of being is painfully shaped between the hammer of experience and the anvil of destiny. Each blow transforms our past and prepares our future. Despite the appalling aspects of suffering, it masks a wisdom which cuts through the skins of our triviality, habit, apathy, and prejudice to reconnect us with our personal reality. Moreover, it represents our personal investment in time and even future stages of our immortality. There are times when we feel absolutely abandoned by fortune, friends, happiness, and love, but we are never deserted by destiny and our spiritual reality.

The desolation wrought by pain can indeed be a midnight hour of impenetrable blackness, but the spark of a new sunrise is always contained within it. In time, suffering purifies, cleanses, corrects, and strengthens as we wrestle to jettison our old selves to release what the Self wills us to become. Of course, all this may sound uplifting, but the coward in me is sorely tempted to be among the first to run for cover and claw an escape through even the thickest brambles. Suffering of any kind casts a fearful shadow, even if it threatens me for my own good. I fear its approach and I implore it to be gentle with me. But it helps to know that it comes as my servant, not my master—and that I have in some mysterious manner called it to me!

First, we have to struggle with the intrusion, the abruptness of the change. There we are moving gently along in calm waters, when suddenly, without warning, we are hurled into churning white water. We become the focus of unalterable circumstances beyond our control or escape. We enter a crisis condition totally unplanned for by the waking mind. We feel instantaneously undone. The ground beneath dissolves, and the old normality of daily life is completely shattered. At such times we are either shocked into anger and rebellion, or cast into a chasm of numbness and paralysis. A crisis compels us to pay attention. We are riveted to the *now*, as past and future rush to the periphery.

Another kind of crisis, often prevalent in biography, is not necessarily marked by a shocking event. This is a kind of creeping paralysis more indicative of gradual and remorseless inner change. In the early stage it may be felt as a discomforting discontent. Old values and conditions become strange and alien, and we become more and more incompatible with ourselves and our surroundings. It is important to realize that every crisis is a process in time; there is a beginning, a middle, and an end. This appreciation can be enormously difficult to sustain, since we feel tyrannized by whirling emotion or, conversely, stuck in the swamps of inaction. All we can do is to set short-term goals using all the will and patience we can muster.

We should also recognize the futility of throwing the blame for our condition on the "enemy," yes, even if we have been mutilated by a drunken driver. Holding deep-seated grudges, spitting forth venom and negativism merely serves to aggravate the situation and delay healing, reconstruction, and reintegration since the soul is preoccupied and smothered by its revenge and bitterness. Somehow we have to draw the strength from deep within to *own* our plight. It happened to us, through us, and, later it may be possible to accept, for us. A real acceptance will in time stir fresh and vigorous forces in the psyche which will alter our relationship to ourselves and the world. Eventually, our crisis will add to our stature, not diminish us, but blame and recrimination sap all our power and creativity, thus hampering our recovery.

Letting go is essential. What we had, what we were, has served its time. It is pointless to waste precious strength trying to hold on to something or someone who has already left, although a proper period of mourning helps us to disentangle ourselves from the past. Fate is deaf; it does no good screaming at it for long. Our initial anger may serve to keep us from being totally submerged, but this, too, will have to be assimilated later on. It is perfectly natural to be angry, but we should not pretend the anger does not exist. We should accept it but prevent it from spilling over into the will and into the world.

Do we see ourselves as victims or as beneficiaries? At first we feel tormented and maltreated, but if we are left with a victim consciousness, we are in real trouble. We will then resist learning what can and should be learned, and thus retard our reintegration with life. We will probably feel intensely alone in our abyss for a while, but aloneness is not the same as loneliness. Aloneness is a temporary state of life, but loneliness is an attitude of soul on which we can work.

What about our relationship to ourselves? Our self-image? It is likely to come under attack in some way. The severity of the assault depends on one's basic perception of oneself. Imbalances and flaws caused by the traumas and abuses of early life will certainly be the target of attack. The introverted psyche, already self-critical, may willingly plunge the dagger of the crisis deeper: "There you are; I knew I was no good. I knew life had it in for me." On the other hand, extroverted personalities will tend to thrash about trying all kinds of futile gyrations to escape, which only makes the situation worse and further upsets the lives of those close to them.

It is important not to confuse our personna-self with who we really are. Previous misdeeds and errors should not disturb the real sanctuary of our being. We may hold a realistic picture of our persona-self and not like the look of it, but this image bears no resemblance to the full vision of our spiritual reality. We just have to learn the lessons the real Self insists we learn. The true wisdom of life has fed us a bitter helping of experience, so we had better pay attention to it. A crisis offers us the opportunity for self-connection and self-correction. Only falling asleep is an affront to this harsh wisdom. We need courage to face it, wisdom to know its benediction, and the strength to endure it.

Crises are direct relatives of those great archetypal crises of birth and death—the great transitions. Each crisis is nothing less and nothing more than the transition between what we were and what we will become. By realizing that a crisis is yet another affirmative demonstration of the I's investment in our growth and destiny, we release fresh and vigorous forces of renewal. Suffering belongs to the spiritual alchemy of creation, as our universe collides with itself to transform its present into future qualities and modes of being. This means that suffering always adds to the meaning and content of destiny; and all past, present, and future adversity represents our investment in our own immortality. I believe we can understand the ultimate meaning of pain only when we develop the vision to acknowledge its dynamic role in the seasons of our immortality. Thus, in the last analysis, the problem is centered in the controversial question of reincarnation.

The longer I live, the more I am astounded by the way people grapple with the obnoxious pressures and conditions threatening to suffocate them. Instead of being driven to pessimism, I marvel at the courage of the human spirit found in the most unlikely places. The slightest possibility that such suffering may be accidental, fruitless, or unjust mocks any thought of a purposeful existence or evolution. Having examined a bit of biography's amazing construction, we should at least be open-minded about destiny and the notion that suffering is meaningful. The next step leads us to consider the thought that our past deeds and experiences may account for some of our present susceptibility to bad health or "misfortune." Nobody questions the fact that too much alcohol can make illness a part of our destiny, but what if we fail to trace the primal source of our phobias, handicaps, and tragedies? Can we not consider the possible existence of a cause planted during an earlier season of our immortality?

Each person's biography is a crowded collage of events, but how many of us are aware of its overall design? At best, we can acknowledge the presence of some unswerving force, a will to survive which may spring from a deep intention to grow and to evolve. This diffused sense of direction trapped somewhere in the unconscious is a whisper we strain to hear, but only feeble echoes reach the waking mind—we just have to trust it. Personal existence contains secrets of immense importance, but they slip through the cracks of reason whenever rational thought tries to grasp them. We may recognize the cryptic outlines of certain patterns and cycles, but most of us are mentally incapable of evaluating our true goals without guidance. We must have passed a milestone or two, but our ultimate aims remain as remote and as unfathomable as ever. Do we need to suffer so much? Conversely, what about those totally unexpected strokes of good fortune, those ecstatic upswings of life's pendulum? Some clamber up the crags of old age with a measure of perspective and wisdom, but are then too weary to turn it to good account! Their lives stand written, and not a line can be erased; they have no more time, energy, or opportunity left for conciliation and reform. Does this mean that death ends their right to grow, their right to heal, their longing to correct old wrongs and errors?

If this world is an arena of experience, being allotted only one entrance and exit is an affront to eternity. After all, how much progress can we be expected to make in one lifetime? An increasing number of people, despite their diverse backgrounds and cultures, acknowledge the idea of reincarnation as a highly relevant and totally sensible concept of human continuity. Despite prejudice and the paucity of convincing evidence, interest in this form of personal evolution persists and even grows in the fertile feelings of the age. Many feel that the sins, errors, inequities, restrictions, and pressing obligations in this life should not bar them from future opportunities for fulfillment. Repelled by the pointless oblivion offered by materialism, they aspire to become creative participants in the unfolding drama of humanity and universe. Knowing there are no easy recipes for salvation, they insist on sharing the long march of becoming. They have no interest in watching the drama of life from celestial couches or languishing in the hopelessness of hell. Thus, there are many who believe that the idea of reincarnation offers a plausible means to value their past, sustain their present, and meet the uncertain future with spiritual confidence. They believe the concept of repeated earth-lives promotes a healthy self-reverence which fortifies the spirit and adds meaning to daily existence and human relationships.

If the great cycles of birth and rebirth turn on the axis of our immortality, our nomadic self must return time and time again to take its pilgrimage through earthly time. Only in this way can we fulfill our potential, correct our errors, and become individuals empowered with freedom. Each expedition is a unique quest for the experiences we must convert into the substance of self-knowing. The Self continually adds to itself through its earthly adventures; its potential is transformed into actual, its imperfection into perfection. This is the rhythmic round of accumulating experience and its transformation into capacity and consciousness.

Without a time structure, biography is nothing more than "a tale told by an idiot, full of sound and fury, signifying nothing." Without destiny, however, time is itself without meaning, while personal evolution without reincarnation is capriciously restricted and undefinable. Finally, reincarnation is meaningless without the greater goals of immortality. But what is the great connecting principle behind all this? One way to approach the dynamic rhythm of birth, death, and rebirth is to consider it as a *process of transformation.*

The Rhythms of Transformation

For the idea of reincarnation to be compatible with my sense of destiny, it must address several fundamental issues. How was this present edition of my life and destiny transcribed from a previous existence? What earlier causes determined my predisposition to health or sickness, my natural talents, and my physical and mental nature? What root causes directed my selection of gender and family, personal relationships, and the locality of my formative years, my culture and race, the historical period I live in? If my immortality is a series of earth appearances, what principles connect all my ends to my beginnings?

Only a serious investigation into the laws of transformation can place reincarnation on a spiritual-scientific footing. Of course, a *direct* study lies beyond the capability of normal thinking. All true examples of transformation, however, contain a universal principle capable of withstanding the light of reason. Not only does every kind of organic life elegantly display such laws in its morphology, but there are also good biographical reasons to assume such laws also regulate the psychological and spiritual development of human beings. Not only do we transform our breakfast into energy and tissue, and our childhood into old age, we also continually absorb experience and convert it into inner capacity and new awareness. We merely extend the range of morphology by asking how our present life will be recast into a new destiny after death and a later rebirth.

The first chapter suggested that human biography can, in some respects, be viewed as an extension, a higher octave, of biology, particularly botany. Mushrooms and babies, ferns and adolescents, grow and develop. All emerge into space and time; all precipitate their material forms according to the time plan orchestrating their developmental patterns. Yes, plant morphology with its rhythmic patterns of transformation offers us a matchless demonstration of the laws of growth.

By following its remarkable sequence of *expansion* and *contraction*, the plant will achieve its goal of fruition and seed production. Stage by ascending stage, the invisible forces of transformation induce greater and greater *refinements* of form and function. Goethe discovered the fact that the leaf is the prototypal organ which is converted into stem, petal, sepal, carpel, stamen, pistil, etc. Plant destiny is a series of births and deaths through which the original seed must die to be reborn. The key to this mystery are the cycles of expansion and contraction, in which the vegetative growth is interrupted and suspended while new refinements of form and function are introduced. These moments reveal phases of interiorization and reorganization which eventually create the super-organized essence, the "idea," of the plants contained in the new seeds.

What magnificent images these are for contemplation! Plant biography is the transformation of form in space and time. Human biography is the transformation of experience into psychological and spiritual growth—in time and space. In the plant, the ubiquitous idea is the *replication* of the species. In us, the idea in action and the motivator behind destiny is the I. In the plant, the contractive phases of interiorization and the production of new organs are its *crises*. In us, these "contractions" are the critical periods between the assimilation of experience and the new impulses released for future change—they are our *crises*. In the plant, the annual "deaths" are seasonal intervals for the interaction of earthly and cosmic forces on the dormant seed. For us, death leads to an interval when the forces of self-transformation are transferred to our spiritual existence before our rebirth. Based on our experience and actions in this life, our post-mortem period will prepare and pre-figure our physical and psychic constitution for our next mortal adventure. Our rebirth is nothing less than another contraction into space and time.

Rudolf Steiner used his highly penetrative clairvoyant insight, applied with rigorous scientific thoroughness, to research the transformations connecting one incarnation to the next. His numerous lectures illustrate how the behavior, attitudes, and actions in one life directly influence the organic and psychological constitution, not to mention the destiny blueprint, of the following life. In other words, the inherent weaknesses and strengths of our present neural, muscular, metabolic, and respiratory systems are largely the highly transmuted result of previous habits, attitudes, and deeds.

Obviously, we need the right kind of physical energy and sentient faculties to achieve the goals set by the I. The idea that our past is imprinted upon our physiognomy, palm prints, heart valves, etc., may seem fanciful, even materialistic, at first. But clearly our corporeal body is the magnificent instrument by which soul and spirit express the themes of our destiny. Could

Rudolf Nureyev dance in the body of George Bernard Shaw, or Sarah Bernhardt speak through the larynx of Madame Curie? The I is incontrovertibly committed to its own progress and the world's evolution—which are one and the same. The plant, on the other hand, is locked into its genetic code season after season. For us, each life will be remarkably different. Although we are rooted in our extensive past, each new birth is a fresh beginning. Time and time again we are free to attract and grasp experience as we ascend the ladder of being and convert potential into actual, imperfection into perfection. This remorseless law insists that every action will create its consequences.

This transformative law of cause and effect is traditionally known by the Hindu word "*karma*." This is no will-o'-the-wisp concept designed to titillate wishful thinking. On the contrary, the idea that we must again and again accept the perils of mortal life demands much personal courage. Knowing, however, that we strive to become ever more human, ever more loving, ever more awake as we grow toward self-knowledge, self-correction, and world service empowers us to drink from the deep wells of spiritual confidence.

Karma invests the word "destiny" with both substance and energy. It also provides a vantage point to overview the tangled web of relationships, commitments, conflicts, disasters, and blessings filling biographical time. Karma is not some dusty theorem retrieved from an ancient crypt nor a credo bound in heavy dogma. It is a living idea offering our mind's-eye view of human existence both range and depth. This law serves the propulsion of the I's drive for growth through experience. It is a spiritual instrument, a tool designed to instruct, to compel us to learn from error and ignorance. Karma organizes our encounters while the I uses it to enlarge its perception of itself, to become its own master. In *Therapeutic Insights, Earthly and Cosmic Laws*, Rudolf Steiner likened karma to a hunger: "The human being, when he is born, *hungers* to do what he does, and he does not give up until he satisfies this hunger. The pressing forward to a karmic event is a result of such a generalized spiritual feeling of hunger."

Above all, karma is through and through a moral law, a spiritually organized system of moral forces. Of course, the mention of morality may lift a brow or two, but karma demonstrates the moral tie between self and world. So often in the ethical clamor of the age we hear it said, "We need a practical solution. It is no good getting stuck in the mire of morality." So many of the modern problems pounding on the doors of conscience show us that the learned ignorance of the times has forgotten the point that *all* the dilemmas of self and world spring from a moral source. Unlike the early civilizations, this one has largely forgotten that the evolution of humankind and universe is designed to run according to the moral principles of the *good and true*.

In general, the major world faiths agree that moral law lies at the very heart of the universal order. But, as morality became deinstitutionalized and destabilized, we became fair game for the skittish political and cultural fashions which manipulate this age. Thus we see an epidemic of moral measles erupting all over the body social. With religious law mostly covered by the concrete of materialism, morality is now a matter between mind and conscience, between the higher and lower qualities of selfhood. It is all grist for the mill of awakening. Now we have mechanistic doctors telling bewildered judges exactly *when* the mechanistic embryo is a being with rights! No matter, the cosmic law holds, and violation of it impedes progress yet sets new energies to work. Injuring others by deed or thought diminishes the self, while virtuous action enhances it. Karma insists that we wound ourselves when we harm others. It is simply the law of consequences working in destiny.

Although we may elude the crude hand of mortal justice, the Self inevitably passes judgement on itself after death. This is the soul realm known traditionally as *Purgatory* in the West and

Kamaloca in the East. This realm is but one phase of our post-mortem existence, where we learn to disconnect ourselves from the clutches of mortal desire and also experience the pain we have brought to others. Here guilt, error, wish, desire, etc., are transmuted into the causative forces which hatch a brand new destiny. Here the longing is aroused to use our return ticket to earth and seek correction, compensation, redemption, and a further advance.

Immoral actions result from distorted or blurry perceptions of the real nature of world and self. But karma turns us toward the light of truth—toward realization and healing. The more our moral center of gravity shifts toward the spiritual reality of our nature, the more the unquenchable moral force of conscience empowers both will and destiny.

The reader considering the idea of reincarnation for the first time may justifiably wonder why this calamitous planet is so important to human development. Why should a spirit wish to exchange its cosmic interlude for another harrowing spell of earthly toil? Why should we not pursue our goals in other spiritual dimensions, in utopias free from fear, pain, divorce, income tax, and perversities? No matter what the compensations and comforts of heaven, Mother Earth offers a wealth of unique experience. Swept along by time, our consciousness of Self shrunken to the pinpoint of the present moment, our past and future lies hidden beyond the horizons of normal awareness. Caught in the coils of time, shuffling through supermarkets, stuck in office or factory, or stationed at the kitchen sink, we appear to be well and truly severed from our cosmic heritage. We peer at the absurdities of life through the narrow filter of the senses, struggle with the resistance of our anatomy and mental and emotional hangups, and try to establish some identity in the ever-shifting social morass. Here impressionable youth is plastered by the commercialism claiming that fulfillment is built on toothpaste, deodorants, or fast cars. They are taught that conduct should conform to the latest fashions of nonconformity while destiny depends on the state of the dollar, the United Nations, or the local legislature! Indeed, we are a long, long way from home, stranded among the legacies of history, taunted by the view that human beings are children of matter—who live only once!

But this seemingly ridiculous muddle offers us the obstructions, the resistance we need to work out destiny and arouse a deeper self-knowledge. We need a body with which to think, feel, and act independently, to know fear, uncertainty, and death. We may compel ourselves to judge our sins and errors after death, but *only on earth can we correct them*, either consciously through our own free efforts, or unconsciously under fate's hammer. Karma implies that all unfulfilled transformation—meaning all uncorrected weaknesses, unused gifts, unpaid debts, guilt, etc.—remain with us. Death removes nothing whatsoever except the opportunity for correction. And so we return. And this is our primal hunger.

Can karma make any sense of history? Can it throw light on what appears to be little more than a huge terrestrial scandal? Can we fit our infinitesimal biography into this enigmatic jigsaw puzzle and find some semblance of personal meaning? From a spiritual mind's-eye, history is far from being a random interplay of individuals, societies, and events. Deep below its chaotic surface runs a subterranean river of evolving, ever-transforming consciousness. It is this rhythmic, flowing stream which carries humanity from egoless primitivity through the great cultural complexes toward higher stages of individuality. Thus the sovereign Self dips itself time and time again into this river of becoming, continually cleansing the past and adding to its treasure of experience and planetary participation.

Karma, woven on the loom of time, reconnects us to those we have known before; through it we engage our race, our nation, and the cultural forces we need to experience. This means that we are old and much-battered residents of history, or better, we *are* history— the transmuted essence of millions of yesterdays, a much-stained litany of follies, invisible violence and shabby transgressions, great aspirations and noble deeds. Did you ever sit on a cool Athenian stone and chuckle while Aristophanes poked fun at Socrates? Did you ever revere a Pharaoh as your God? Did you choke on the dust of a Crusade, or smell your own incineration on a medieval pyre? Whatever the case, history has fashioned the substance of your present reality, and, somewhere in time, redemption will break all shackles forged in time past. This means that those trampled into the muds of battle, those who fell by the wayside of great migrations, those herded into slavery, are never lost, never obliterated. They fall in one age to be reborn in another. Not a particle of experience is lost, and the poisoned ground of Auschwitz will be reploughed. The law of the conservation of experience means that all is transformed, never lost, mislaid, dispersed. Where there is karma there is redemption. This is no circular sorrow-go-round, but rather an ascending spiral of fulfillment. Karma makes poetry of the brutal prose of history.

Final Thoughts—The Sense of Destiny

This book has attempted to illustrate how a serious examination of biography reveals a rich array of rhythmic and transformational phenomena. At best, it is little more than a preliminary survey, a mere fraction of the research done by myself and by others. For the sake of brevity, I have omitted the well documented eighteen-year cycle, the thirty-three-year rhythm discovered by Rudolf Steiner, the force behind the genesis of karma, the causal threads between the first and second halves of life, and much more. Only an esoteric evaluation of such phenomena in terms of human nature and its spiritual activity before birth and after death will fully illuminate the generation of destiny. I do hope, however, that I have disclosed enough to prompt some readers to draw up their own time charts. Such an exercise will more than likely uncover the presence of the wisdom which makes biography such a miraculous work of art. I also hope this introduction underlines the precious need to develop a proper morphology of biography to be placed at the service of those who counsel, educate, and heal. To imbue the word "destiny" with both validity and personal power we must perceive the time fabric of biography and then study it as a process of transformation from both phenomenological and spiritual vantage points. This kind of examination is essentially a union of analysis and synthesis.

Each of us possess our unique frame of reference—our own life story. By looking at it carefully we can measure and arrange all our bits and pieces of the symmetry of truth. Then we have an overview permitting us to peer over the wasteland of meaninglessness and accident to see a heart-sustaining glimpse of our own spiritual wisdom. Where we saw chaos, we now see *organization*. To suffer from meaninglessness, to see oneself twitching on the strings of circumstance, is the most tragic and debilitating malaise of this age. Only a sense of destination gives the soul a spiritual anchorage in the maelstrom of these times. Souls who recognize destiny and freedom will never be fugitives from fate.

Looking at biography as destiny and transformation helps us appreciate just how profoundly committed we are to our own life and the lives of others. A sense of destiny allows us to look beyond the character traits and lifestyles of our fellows, because we know they are greater than they appear to be in the present moment. Sensing the unique destiny of the other is a recognition of the singular reality of each *Thou* we come across in life. Such a perception can only enrich our power of communication. Wordsworth was correct when he said, "We are greater than we know."

A sense of destiny not only alters our attitude to life, it also changes the connection between the waking mind and the hidden levels of the psyche. Thus we develop an absolutely new awareness of time, and an exalted sense of time as *new consciousness*. We too easily forget that everything has its share of time, its seasons of becoming, from the humble worm to civilizations and solar systems. Whenever we feel impatient, we should remember that destiny decrees times of increase and times of decrease, times of action and times of assimilation. Thus, this added dimension of awareness permits us to look beyond temporality to the "forever."

Think, then, of living in time as *filling in eternity*. Moment by moment, we select for action some of the possibilities swarming out of the future, thereby adding more and more experiential gold to the treasure house we call the "past." But we never lose this past. It lives. It *is*. The finite content of a single moment, a single decision, a single lifetime, has meaning only in the context of the all-embracing whole. Destiny, then, is the process whereby we gradually fill eternity and make it *personal*. By uncovering the veiled pulse of time we can understand the dialogue between self, world, and cosmos. If we feel this task is beyond our present power, we can at least pay greater attention to the particular page we compose in each "now."

Background Reading

Blair, Lawrence. *Rhythms of Vision*. London: Paladin, 1976.

Bleibtreu, John. *The Parable of the Beast*. London: Paladin, 1970.

Bunning, E. *The Psychological Clock*. New York: Academic Press, 1964.

Burckhardt, Titus. *Alchemy*, trans. William Stoddart. London: Stuart and Watkins, 1967.

Chardin, Teilard de, "Mon Univers" (1924) in *Science et Christ*, ed. du Seuil, vol.ix.

Clark, Ronald W. *Einstein: The Life and Times*. New York and Cleveland: World Publishing, 1971.

Cloudsley-Thompson, J.L. *Rhythmic Activity in Animal Physiology and Behavior*. New York: Academic Press, 1961.

Curie, Eve. *Madame Curie*. New York: Doubleday & Co., 1938.

Darwin, Charles. *Autobiography and Selected Letters*, edited by Francis Darwin. New York: Dover, 1958.

Dewey, Edward R. and Mandino, Og. *Cycles*. New York: Hawthorn, 1971.

Dunne, John. *The Serial Universe*. London: Faber and Faber Limited, 1934.

——*An Experiment with Time*. Faber and Faber Limited, 1939.

Eliade, Mircea. *Myth and Reality*. New York and Evanston: Harper & Row, Harper Torchbooks, 1968.

Fagan, Cyril. *Astrological Origins*. St. Paul, Minnesota: Llewellyn Publications, 1971.

Frankl, Victor E. *The Doctor and the Soul, from Psychotherapy to Logotherapy*. New York: Bantam Books, 1967.

Frank, Anne. *The Diary of a Young Girl*, rev. ed., Mooryart. New York: Doubleday, 1967.

Fraser, J.T., ed., *The Voice of Time*. New York: George Braziller, 1966.

Gauquelin, Michael. *Cosmic Clocks: From Astrology to Modern Science*. New York: Avon Books, 1969.

Gleadow, Robert. *The Origin of the Zodiac*. New York: Atheneum, 1969.

Harwood, A.C. *The Way of A Child*. London: Rudolf Steiner Press, 1988.

Henderson, Joseph L. and Oakes, Maude. *The Wisdom of the Serpent*. New York, 1963.

Heuscher, Julius E. *A Psychiatric Study of Fairy Tales: Their Origin, Meaning and Usefulness*. Springfield, IL: Charles Thomas, 1947.

Jung, C.G. *The Collected Works of C.G. Jung: The Structure and Dynamics of the Psyche*. New York: Pantheon Books, 1960.

——*Memories, Dreams, and Reflections*. Vintage Books rev. ed. New York: Random House, Inc., 1965.

——*Synchronicity: An Acausal Connecting Principle*. Bollingen Series LI. New York: Pantheon Books, 1955.

James, William. *The Letters of William James*. Boston: Little, Brown and Company, 1920.

Keller, Helen. *The Story of My Life*. London: Hodder and Stoughton, 1904.

King, Coretta. *My Life with Martin Luther King*. New York: Holt, Rinehart and Winston, 1969.

Koestler, Arthur. *The Roots of Coincidence*. New York: Vintage Books, 1973.

——*The Act of Creation*. New York: Laurel Edition, Dell Publishing, 1967.

——*The Sleepwalkers*. London: Hutchinson, 1959.

König, Karl, *The First Three Years of the Child*. New York: Anthroposophic Press, 1984.

Lehrs, Ernst. *Man or Matter*. London: Rudolf Steiner Press, 1985..

Lewis, C.S. *The Problem of Pain*. NewYork: Collins/Fontana Books, 1973.

Lissau, Rudi. *Rudolf Steiner: Life, Work, Inner Path and Social Initiatives*. Stroud, England: Hawthorn Press, 1987.

Luce, Gay Gaer. *Biological Rhythms in Human and Animal Physiology*. New York: Dover, 1971.

——*Body Time: Physiological Rhythms and Social Stress*. New York: Pantheon Books, 1971.

Manuel, Frank. *A Portrait of Isaac Newton*. Cambridge: Harvard University Press, 1968.

McDermott, Robert A. *The Essential Steiner*. New York: HarperCollins Publishers, 1984.

Milne, Lorus and Margery. *The Senses of Animals and Man*. London: Andre Deutsche, 1964.

Michell, John. *City of Revelation*. London: Garnstone Press, 1972.

Nicoll, Maurice. *Living Time*. London: Vincent Stuart, 1952.

Payne, Robert. *Lawrence of Arabia*. London: Robert Hale, 1962.

Perry, Ralph Barton. *The Thought and Character of William James*, 2 vols. Boston: Little, Brown and Co.,1935.

Priestley, J.B. *Man and Time*, Laurel edition. New York: Dell Publishing Company, 1968.

Progoff, Ira. *Jung, Synchronicity and Human Destiny*. New York: Julian Press, 1973.

Roosevelt, Eleanor. *Autobiography*. Harper and Brothers, 1958

Santillana, Georgio de, and Dechend. *Hertha von Hamlet's Mill*. Boston: Gambit, 1969.

Sears, Paul B. *Charles Darwin: The Naturalist as a Cultural Force*. Charles Scribner's, 1950.

Smuts, Johann Christian. *Holism and Evolution*. London: Macmillan, 1926.

Steiner, Rudolf. *The Search for the New Isis, The Divine Sophia*. Spring Valley, N.Y.: Mercury Press, 1983.

——*Ancient Myths: Their Meaning and Connection with Evolution*, new ed. forthcoming. Hudson, N.Y.: Anthroposophic Press, 1994.

——*The Evolution of Consciousness*. Sussex, England: Rudolf Steiner Press, 1991.

——*The Karma of Vocation*. Hudson, N.Y.: Anthroposophic Press, 1984.

—— *The Manifestations of Karma.* Bristol, England: Rudolf Steiner Press, 1992.

——*The Philosophy of Spiritual Activity.* Hudson, N.Y.: Anthroposophic Press, 1986.

—— *The Study of Man.* London: Rudolf Steiner Press, 1984.

—— *Therapeutic Insights, Earthly and Cosmic Laws.* Spring Valley, N.Y.: Mercury Press, 1984.

Sweeney, Beatrice M. *Rhythmic Phenomena in Plants.* London and New York: Academic Press, 1969.

Thomas, M. *Alexander von Humboldt: Scientist, Explorer, Adventurer.* Pantheon Books, 1960.

Troyat, Henri. *Tolstoy,* trans. Nancy Amphous. Garden City, N.Y.: Doubleday & Company, Inc.

——*Firebrand: The Life of Dostoevsky.* trans. Norbert Gyterman. New York: Roy Publishers, 1946.

Trives, Eleanor. *The Sun's Path,* edited by Firmin-Didot, Imprimeurs de l'Institut de France.

van der Post, Laurens. *The Heart of the Hunter.* New York: William Morrow and Company, 1968.

——*The Dark Eye of Africa.* New York: William Morrow, 1955.

Watson, E.L. Grant. *The Mystery of Physical Life.* Hudson, N.Y.: Lindisfarne Press, 1992.

Wells, Geoffrey H. *Charles Darwin: A Portrait.* Yale University Press, 1938.

Whitrow, G.J. *What Is Time?* London: Thames and Hudson, 1972.

Zweig, Stefan. *Balzac.* New York: Viking Press, 1946.

WILLIAM BRYANT

was born in 1933, and raised in the West Country of England. Trained as an aircraft engineer, he has devoted the past thirty-five years to Waldorf education in South Africa, Europe, and the United States. Presently, he lives in Gig Harbor, Washington.